38067100540772

Original text by Tony Kelly
Revised and updated by Robin McKelvie and Jenny McKelvie

First published 2008. Information revised and updated 2012
ISBN: 978-0-7495-7081-1

Published by AA Publishing, a trading name of AA Media Limited, whose registered office is Fanum House, Basing View, Basingstoke, Hampshire RG21 4EA.
Registered number 06112600.

A CIP catalogue record for this book is available from the British Library

The content of this book is believed to be accurate at the time of printing. Due to its nature the content is likely to vary or change and the publisher is not responsible for such change and accordingly is not responsible for the consequences of any reliance by the reader on information that has changed. Any rights that are given to consumers under applicable law are not affected. Opinions expressed are for guidance only and are those of the assessor based on their experience at the time of review and may differ from the reader's opinions based on their subsequent experience. We have tried to ensure accuracy in this guide, but things do change, so please let us know if you have any comments at travelguides@theAA.com.

Colour separation: AA Digital Department
Printed and bound in Italy by Printer Trento S.r.l.

Find out more about AA Publishing and the wide range of services the AA provides by visiting our website at theAA.com/shop

A04463
Maps produced from map data supplied by Global Mapping, Brackley, UK.
Transport map © Communicarta Ltd, UK

About this book

Symbols are used to denote the following categories:

- map reference to maps on cover
- address or location
- telephone number
- opening times
- admission charge
- restaurant or cafe on premises or nearby
- nearest underground train station
- nearest bus/tram route
- nearest overground train station
- nearest ferry stop
- nearest airport
- other practical information
- tourist information office
- ➤ indicates the page where you will find a fuller description

This book is divided into five sections.

Maps
All map references are to the maps on the covers. For example, Pula Arena has the reference 2E – indicating the grid square in which it is to be found

Admission prices
Inexpensive (under 20kn)
Moderate (20–40kn)
Expensive (over 40kn)

Hotel prices
Price are per room per night, including breakfast:
€ budget (under 500kn); **€€** moderate (500–1,000kn); **€€€** expensive (over 1,000kn)

Restaurant prices
Price for a three-course meal per person without drinks: **€** budget (under 100kn); **€€** moderate (100–200kn);
€€€ expensive (over 200kn)

Contents

The essence of...

From the eastern plains of Slavonia to the fashionable Adriatic coast, Croatia is a fascinating blend of Balkan, central European and Mediterranean cultures. This is a country which has taken on influences from Venice to Vienna and Belgrade to Istanbul, and moulded them to create a distinct national character. The people of Croatia are patriotic but welcoming to strangers, proud of their history yet open to new ideas. Despite the traumas of their recent past, they have a relaxed Mediterranean attitude to life and like nothing better than to sit outside a cafe with friends.

features

It has more than a thousand islands, a beautiful coastline and the cleanest waters in the Mediterranean. It has mountains, lakes, waterfalls, rivers, buzzing cities and historic Venetian towns. In short, it has everything you could want on a holiday.

Before 1990, crowds flocked to the Adriatic beaches of what was then part of Yugoslavia. Then along came the wars that tore Yugoslavia apart, and Croatia disappeared off the tourist map. The majority of the coastal resorts were unaffected by the fighting but people saw a country at war and stayed away.

Croatia these days is firmly back on the tourist circuit and indeed has emerged as one of the Mediterranean's brightest rising stars. There are few visible signs of damage in the country, unless you choose to venture inland to the border areas of Slavonia and Dalmatia. Forced to rebuild its tourist industry from scratch, Croatia has learned from the mistakes of the past. Golf courses, marinas and cycle routes are being developed; the new trends are towards rural tourism and family-run hotels as Croatia rejects "hamburgerization" and embraces a future that puts quality firmly before quantity.

Croatia has also become increasingly popular with the international jet set, with royalty and film stars regularly dropping by on their yachts. This is a young, confident country, that is proud of where it is at and is looking to embrace the European family of nations even more as it continues its work towards becoming a member of the European Union.

PEOPLE

- Croatia has a population of just under 4.5 million people, according to the latest census.
- Zagreb, the capital, has a population of almost a million. The next biggest cities are Split, Rijeka, Osijek and Zadar.
- Around 90 per cent of the population are ethnic Croats and 5 per cent are Serbs.
- Religion is divided along ethnic lines; 88 per cent are Roman Catholic and 4 per cent Serbian Orthodox.

GEOGRAPHY

- Croatia has 5,835km (3,626 miles) of coastline, of which 4,058km (2,522 miles) is on islands and 1,777km (1,104 miles) on the mainland.
- There are 1,185 islands, of which about 50 are inhabited.
- The highest mountain is Dinara (1,831m/6,007ft), on the Bosnian border near Knin.
- The longest river is the Sava, which runs for 562km (350 miles) across Croatia.

food & drink

Croatian cooking is rooted in historical and geographical influences, and broadly divided into two distinct styles. The cuisine of the Adriatic coast is based on fresh fish and seafood, together with pasta and risotto, legacies of Italian and Venetian rule. By contrast, the cuisine of the continental regions is heavier and spicier, with dishes such as goulash betraying a central European influence.

STARTERS AND SNACKS

Almost every menu begins with *pršut* (cured ham, similar to an Italian prosciutto) and *paški sir* (sheep's cheese from the island of Pag), which, together with bread and olives, make the perfect starter. Pasta and risotto dishes are usually listed as "warm starters"; a speciality is *crni rižot* (black risotto with cuttlefish ink). The popular national snack is *ćevapčići*, which is a kind of grilled meatball usually served with raw onions, *ajvar* (aubergine and pepper relish) and crusty bread. Alternatives include *pljeskavica* (hamburger) and *ražnjići* (kebabs). For a cheap snack, bakeries sell *burek* (filo pastry with minced meat or cheese).

REGIONAL SPECIALITIES

In Istria, look out for local truffles, served in numerous ways but most commonly with steak, omelettes or pasta. Dalmatian dishes include *brodet* (fish casserole) and *pasticada* (beef stewed with sweet wine and served with gnocchi). Also popular along the coast is meat cooked under a *peka*, a metal lid which is covered with hot embers. Specialities of the Zagorje, north of Zagreb, include *štrukli*

(cottage cheese ravioli) and *purica z mlincima* (turkey with pasta).

The eastern region of Slavonia produces famously spicy food, such as *kulen* (paprika-flavoured salami), *gulaš* (goulash), *čobanec* (meat stew), *fiš paprikaš* (fish stew) and boiled beef with horseradish.

The mountain regions have their own cuisine, with hearty dishes reflecting the harsh climate. These include *grah* (bean stew with sausages), *janjetina* (spit-roast lamb) and game, which might be venison, wild boar or occasionally bear.

MAIN COURSES

Grilled meat features on most menus, either as steak or schnitzels such as *zagrebački odrezak* (breaded veal stuffed with ham and cheese). Fish is usually plain grilled, and is often accompanied by *blitva* (spinach) and potatoes. Vegetables and salads are listed separately on the menu and generally include chips, rice, cabbage and beetroot salad.

DESSERTS

The most popular dessert is *palačinke* (pancakes filled with walnuts, chocolate or jam). Dalmatia produces *rožata*, which is similar to a *crème caramel*. The Croatians love *sladoled* (ice cream), which is sold all over the country in a huge variety of flavours.

WINES, BEERS AND SPIRITS

Croatia produces some excellent wines. The best red wines are Dingač and Postup from the Pelješac Peninsula near Dubrovnik. White wines to look out for include Malvazija from Istria, Graševina from Slavonia, Grk and Pošip from Korčula and Vugava from Vis. *Prošek* is a sweet red wine from Dalmatia.

Lager-type beers include Karlovačko and Ožujsko. Strong brandy and spirits are often drunk either before or after a meal. The general term for these is *rakija*; popular varieties include *šlijvovica* (plum brandy), *lozovaca* (grape brandy), *travarica* (herb brandy) and *biska* (mistletoe brandy from Istria).

short break

If you only have a short time to visit Croatia, or would like to get a really complete picture of the country, here are the essentials:

- **Go island-hopping in the Adriatic** using the excellent network of ferries – better still, rent your own yacht.

- **Soak up the laid-back atmosphere** and baroque architecture of Croatia's inland towns such as Varaždin (➤ 52) and Samobor (➤ 145).

- **Take a walk around Dubrovnik's city walls,** then plunge into the medieval streets of the old town, with its beautifully restored churches, fountains and palaces (➤ 40).

- **Take in a performance** during one of the summer festivals in Dubrovnik, Split and towns along the coast (➤ 68).

- **Sample fresh truffles in the hill towns of inland Istria** (➤ 185), then head down to the coast for an evening by the sea in pretty-as-a-picture Rovinj (➤ 50).

- **Sip chilled *prošek* or *malvazija* wine** on a summer evening by the sea, then dine on simply grilled fresh fish at a harbourside restaurant.

• **Spend a day admiring the scenery of the Plitvice Lakes** (➤ 46–47) or Krka National Park (➤ 100), with their stunning emerald-green waterfalls, rivers and lakes.

• **Take off all your clothes** and dress as nature intended on one of Croatia's nudist beaches – everyone else does it, and you will never get a better chance.

• **Have coffee in Trg Bana Jelačića in Zagreb** (➤ 133), then take the funicular to Gornji Grad (➤ 38) to explore the oldest part of the city.

• **Play gladiators in the Roman arena at Pula** (➤ 48) – if you can, go to a concert here.

Planning

ULAZ
1
STOP
UZMITE KARTICU
SELF TICKETING

Before you go

WHEN TO GO

JAN	FEB	MAR	APR	MAY	JUN	JUL	AUG	SEP	OCT	NOV	DEC
11°C	12°C	14°C	17°C	21°C	25°C	28°C	28°C	25°C	21°C	16°C	13°C
52°F	54°F	57°F	63°F	70°F	77°F	82°F	82°F	77°F	70°F	61°F	55°F

High season　Low season

The temperatures above are the average daily maximum for Dubrovnik. Temperatures are similar along the Adriatic coast. Sunshine is almost guaranteed throughout the summer, particularly during the peak holiday season of July and August. If you want to avoid the crowds but still enjoy warm, sunny weather, the best months are May, June and September. Between October and April, many hotels close their doors, and resorts which are lively in summer have a distinct off-season feel. Zagreb, Split and Dubrovnik are busy throughout the year. Away from the coast, the weather is cooler and more unpredictable. You should always take warm clothes and be prepared for wind, rain and snow in mountain areas, especially in winter.

WHAT YOU NEED

● Required
○ Suggested
▲ Not required

Some countries require a passport to remain valid for a minimum period (usually at least six months) beyond the date of entry – contact their consulate or embassy or your travel agency for details.

	UK/ireland	USA/Canada	Australia	New Zealand	EU countries
Passport valid for 6 months beyond date of departure/national ID card	●	●	●	●	●
Visa (regulations can change – check before booking your trip)	▲	▲	▲	▲	▲
Onward or return ticket	○	○	○	○	○
Health inoculations (polio, tetanus, typhoid, hepatitis A)	○	○	○	○	○
Health documentation (➤ 23, Health Insurance)	▲	▲	▲	▲	▲
Travel insurance	○	○	○	○	○
Driving licence (current national or international)	●	●	●	●	●
Car insurance certificate (if own car)	●	●	●	●	●
Car registration document (if own car)	●	●	●	●	●

WEBSITES

www.croatia.hr (Croatian National Tourist Board)
www.croatiatraveller.com (online guide)
www.croatiaairlines.com (Croatia airlines)
www.jadrolina.hr (ferry routes and timetables)

TOURIST OFFICES AT HOME

In the UK

Croatian National Tourist Office
2 The Lanchesters
162–164 Fulham Palace Road
London, W6 9ER
☎ 020 8563 7979

In the US

Croatian National Tourist Office
350 Fifth Avenue
Suite 4003
New York, NY 10118
☎ 212/279-8672

On the Web

Tourist information on Croatia is available in Croatian, English and German on the Croatian National Tourist Board website at www.croatia.hr.

HEALTH INSURANCE

Although not yet a member of the EU, Croatia offers citizens of European Union countries free emergency medical treatment on production of their passport. This covers essential hospital stays, but excludes some expenses such as the cost of prescribed medicines. Private medical insurance is still advised and is essential for all other visitors.

Dental treatment has to be paid for by all visitors but is usually covered by private medical insurance.

TIME DIFFERENCES

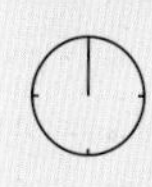

Netherlands
1PM

Croatia is on Central European Time, one hour ahead of Greenwich Mean Time. Summer time (GMT+2) operates from the last Sunday in March to the last Sunday in October.

NATIONAL HOLIDAYS

1 Jan *New Year's Day*
6 Jan *Epiphany*
Mar/Apr *Easter Monday*
1 May *Labour Day*
May/Jun *Corpus Christi*
22 Jun *Anti-Fascist Resistance Day*
25 Jun *Croatian National Day*
5 Aug *Victory Day*
15 Aug *Feast of the Assumption*
8 Oct *Independence Day*
1 Nov *All Saints' Day*
25–26 Dec *Christmas*

WHAT'S ON WHEN

Every town and city in Croatia has its own annual feast day, held in honour of their patron saint or to commemorate a historic victory over the Turks. Celebrations are usually a mix of religious and secular, with processions, Masses, fireworks, music, dancing and crowds in traditional folk costume. In Slavonia, you will see people dancing the *kolo* (circle dance) to the sound of the *tamburica* (mandolin), while in Dalmatia you may hear a *klapa* (male voice choir). Details are available from local tourist offices.

February/March *St Blaise (3 February):* large procession in Dubrovnik in honour of the city's patron saint, whose relics are carried around the old town.
Carnival (February/March): the pre-Lenten Carnival is celebrated across the country. The biggest parade takes place in Rijeka on the Sunday before Shrove Tuesday.

March/April *Good Friday:* religious processions in Korčula and in the villages around Jelsa on Hvar.
St Vincent (28 April): the Kumpanija sword dance is performed in the village of Blato on Korčula (www.korculainfo.com).

May *St Domnius (7 May):* feast day celebrated in Split in honour of the patron saint.

Rab Tournament (9 May): re-enactment of a medieval tournament in Rab, in which knights fight each other with crossbows.
Festival Tamburaške Glazbe (late May): a week of concerts of *tamburica* (mandolin) music in Osijek.

June *Brodsko Kolo (mid-June):* Croatia's oldest and biggest traditional folklore festival takes place in Slavonski Brod, with music, dancing, folk costume and parades of wedding carriages (www.brodsko-kolo.com).

July *Dakovacki Vezovi (first weekend):* "Dakovo Embroidery" is a celebration of Slavonian folk culture, with *tamburica* music, dancing and displays of gypsy wagons and horses.
Rab Tournament (27 July): re-enactment of a medieval tournament in Rab, in which knights fight each other with crossbows.
St Theodor (29 July): performances of the Moreška sword dance in Korčula (www.korculainfo.com).

August *Sinjska Alka (first Sunday):* medieval jousting by horsemen in cavalry uniform in the Dalmatian town of Sinj.
Trka Na Prstenac (mid-August): displays of horsemanship at the "Tilting at the Ring" festival in the Istrian town of Barban.
Assumption (15 August): large pilgrimage to Marija Bistrica. Another takes place on 8 September to mark the birth of the Virgin.

September *Špancirfest (late August/early September):* 10 days of open-air concerts and street entertainment in Varaždin (www.spancirfest.com).
Marco Polo (early September): A re-enactment of the naval battle of 1298 between Venetian and Genoese fleets in which Marco Polo was captured takes place in Korčula around the anniversary of the battle on 7 September.
Subotina (second weekend): Folk festival in the Istrian hill town of Buzet to mark the start of the truffle season, including the world's biggest truffle omelette (www.buzet.hr).
Ilok Wine Fair (second or third Saturday): annual grape fair in Ilok, a small town on the River Danube near Vukovar, to celebrate the wine harvest, with *tamburica* music, folk dancing and local wine (www.turizamilok.hr).
St Euphemia (16 September): feast day in Rovinj in honour of the patron saint.

Getting there

BY AIR

Zagreb (Pleso) Airport

17km (10.5 miles) to city centre

N/A

30 minutes

15 minutes

Dubrovnik Airport

20km (12 miles) to city centre

N/A

30 minutes

30 minutes

There are international airports at Dubrovnik, Zagreb, Split, Pula, Rijeka and Zadar. Croatia Airlines operates flights to Zagreb from most major European capitals. Ferries from Italy arrive at Zadar, Split and Dubrovnik, with additional services to Istria and to the main islands in summer. Buses and trains from central Europe arrive in Zagreb. You can drive into Croatia from Slovenia, Hungary, Serbia, Bosnia-Herzegovina and Montenegro.

AIRPORT TRANSFERS

There are regular shuttle buses from Zagreb airport to the city centre. Buses depart every 30–60 minutes throughout the day and terminate beside the central bus station. Shuttle buses from other airports are timed to coincide with the arrival of incoming flights. Taxis are also available at all airports.

Getting around

PUBLIC TRANSPORT

Buses Buses are generally the easiest way to get around, with an extensive network of services connecting the main towns, cities and resorts. In big cities such as Zagreb, you should buy your ticket in advance from the ticket windows at the main bus station. On local and island routes, you can buy your ticket on the bus.

Trains The rail network covers most major cities with the exception of Dubrovnik. High-speed tilting trains, equipped with personal headphones and laptop connections, operate on the route from Zagreb to Split, with a journey time of five hours.

Urban transport Larger cities such as Zagreb, Split and Dubrovnik have their own municipal bus services. Tickets are available from the driver but are cheaper if bought in advance from newspaper kiosks. Tickets must be validated in the machine beside the driver as you board. Zagreb also has an efficient network of trams, and a funicular railway between the upper and lower towns. The Zagreb Card, available from tourist offices, gives unlimited access to public transport for 72 hours

Ferries Car and passenger ferries between islands and the mainland are operated by Jadrolinija. There is also a regular car ferry along the Adriatic coast from Rijeka to Dubrovnik, stopping at Zadar, Split, Hvar, Korčula and Mljet. There is no system of reservations for local ferries, so you should arrive at the harbour well in advance, particularly if you are travelling by car. Timetables and fares are available at all ferry ports or at www.jadrolinija.hr.

TAXIS

Taxis can be hired from cab ranks in Zagreb and other main towns. Taxi ranks can usually be found at bus and train stations and ferry ports. Fares are metered, with supplements for late-night travel and at weekends, and an additional charge payable for luggage.

DRIVING

- Speed limit on motorways (*autocesta* – toll payable): 130kph (80mph)
- Speed limit on main roads: 110kph (68mph)

- Speed limit on minor roads 90kph (56mph)
- Speed limit on urban roads: 50kph (31mph)
- Seat belts must be worn at all times. Children under 12 must sit in the back seat.
- The use of mobile phones while driving is forbidden.
- Headlights must be switched on at all times.
- The drink-drive limit is zero and is strictly enforced.
- Fuel is sold in various grades, including Eurosuper 95, Super 98 and Eurodiesel. Petrol stations are usually open 7am–8pm (7am–10pm in summer), on motorways and major roads they are open 24 hours.
- If you are driving your own car in Croatia, you should take out European breakdown cover before you leave. Roadside assistance is provided by the Hrvatski Autoklub (tel: 987) according to a fixed scale of charges. Car rental firms will provide their own rescue service.

CAR RENTAL

The leading international car rental companies have offices at the main airports. There are also local companies in all major resorts. Keep your hire documents, passport and driving licence with you at all times, and never leave them unattended in the car.

FARES AND TICKETS

Long-distance buses are operated by numerous private companies and tickets are not transferable, so make sure your ticket is valid for the bus you want to catch. Return fares are cheaper but mean travelling with the same company in both directions. On buses and trains, children under 12 generally travel half-price and children under four travel free.

Students Holders of an International Student Identity Card (ISIC) may be able to obtain discounts on public transport and entrance fees. There are youth hostels affiliated with Hostelling International in Zagreb, Pula, Zadar, Rijeka, Veli, Losinj, Zadštrog, Gradac and Dubrovnik, with discounts for students, people under 26 and members of hostelling organizations (see www.hfhs.hr).

Senior citizens Travellers over 60 are generally entitled to reduced fares on public transport and reduced entrance fees at museums.

Children Children under 12 travel half-price on most buses, trains and ferries, while children under three or four travel free of charge.

Being there

TOURIST OFFICES

Zagreb
Trg Bana Jelačića 11
☎ 01 481 4051
www.zagreb-touristinfo.hr

Dubrovnik
Brsaije 5
☎ 020 312011
www.tzdubrovnik.hr

Hvar
Trg Svetog Stjepana
☎ 021 741059
www.hvar.hr

Opatija
Ulica Vladimira Nazora 3
☎ 051 271710
www.opatija-tourism.hr

Poreč
Zagrebačka 9
☎ 052 451293
www.istra.hr

Pula
Forum 3
☎ 052 219197
www.istra.hr

Rab
Trg Municipium Arba 8
☎ 051 724064
www.tzg-rab.hr

Rijeka
Korzo 33
☎ 051 335882
www.tz-rijeka.hr

Rovinj
Obala Pina Budicina 12
☎ 052 811566
www.tzgrovinj.hr

Split
Peristil ☎ 021 345606
www.visitsplit.com

Varaždin
Ulica Ivana Padovca 3
☎ 042 210987
www.tourism-varazdin.hr

Zadar
Ilije Smiljanica 5
☎ 023 316166
www.tzzadar.hr

There are tourist information offices in all main towns and resorts, though some are only open in summer, particularly on the islands. Opening hours are 8 or 9–5 or 6 (reduced hours on Sunday and often closed for lunch in smaller offices). Staff are multilingual and can generally issue free maps and guides. Local travel agencies such as Atlas have offices in all the main towns and are good sources of information and private rooms.

Tourist information in English, German and Italian is available in Croatia from April to October. Call Croatian Angels (tel: 062 999999).

MONEY

Croatia's currency is the kuna (kn), which is divided into 100 lipa. Coins are issued in denominations of 1, 2, 5, 10, 20 and 50 lipa, 1kn, 2kn and 5kn. Notes are issued in denominations of 5, 10, 20, 50, 100, 200, 500 and 1,000kn. The euro is widely accepted and accommodation prices are often quoted in both euros and kuna.

Credit cards are widely used. You can withdraw money from ATM (cashpoint) machines using a credit or debit card with a PIN (personal identification number).

TIPS/GRATUITIES

Yes ✓ No ✕

Restaurants	✓	10%
Cafés/bars	✓	change
Tour guides	✓	10–20kn
Taxis	✓	10%
Porters	✓	10kn
Chambermaids	✓	10kn
Toilets	✕	

POSTAL AND INTERNET SERVICES

Main post offices are open from Monday to Friday 7am–7pm, and on Saturday mornings. In smaller towns and on islands, they may be open on weekday mornings only. The post office next to the railway station in Zagreb is open 24 hours. Stamps can be bought at post offices and news kiosks.

Internet access is often available in larger towns and resorts, in the form of Internet cafes or cafes and bars with WiFi. Hotels often have a PC that is wired up to the Internet for guests to use, some also provide in-room Internet services in the form of hardwire connections or WiFi.

TELEPHONES

There are public telephones in all main towns and resorts. Phonecards *(telefonska kartica)* can be bought at post offices, newsagents and kiosks. Mobile phone coverage is almost universal; make sure your phone is switched to international roaming before you go. The international dialling code for Croatia is tel: 385.

International dialling codes
from Croatia to:
UK: ☎ 00 44
USA/Canada: ☎ 00 1
Ireland: ☎ 00 353
Australia: ☎ 00 61

Emergency telephone numbers
Police: ☎ 92
Fire: ☎ 93
Ambulance: ☎ 94

EMBASSIES AND CONSULATES

UK: ☎ 01 600 9100; http://ukincroatia.fco.gov.uk
US: ☎ 01 661 2200; http://zagreb.usembassy.gov
Australia: ☎ 01 489 1200; www.auembassy.hr
Germany: ☎ 01 630 0100; www.zagreb.diplo.de
Ireland: ☎ 01 631 0025

HEALTH ADVICE

Sun advice The sun is intense on the Adriatic coast in summer and it is possible to burn very quickly. Cover up with a high-factor sunscreen, wear a hat and drink plenty of water. Children are especially vulnerable and need to be protected, especially when playing near the sea.

Drugs Prescription and non-prescription drugs and medicines are available from pharmacies *(ljekarna)*. Outside normal hours, a notice on the door of each pharmacy should give the address of the nearest duty chemist. Take adequate supplies of any drugs that you need regularly as they may not be available. Other items to consider include insect repellent, anti-diarrhoea pills and sea-sickness tablets.

PERSONAL SAFETY

Violence against tourists is unusual. Theft from cars is the most common form of crime.

- Do not leave valuables on the beach or poolside.
- Always lock valuables in hotel safety deposit boxes.
- Never leave anything inside your car. If you have to, lock it out of sight in the boot.
- Beware of pickpockets in crowded markets, and on buses and trams in Dubrovnik, Split and Zagreb.
- Police assistance: tel: 92 from any phone.

ELECTRICITY

The power supply is 220 volts AC. Sockets take two-pronged round continental plugs. Visitors from the UK will need an adaptor and visitors from the USA will require a transformer for appliances operating on 100–120 volts.

OPENING HOURS

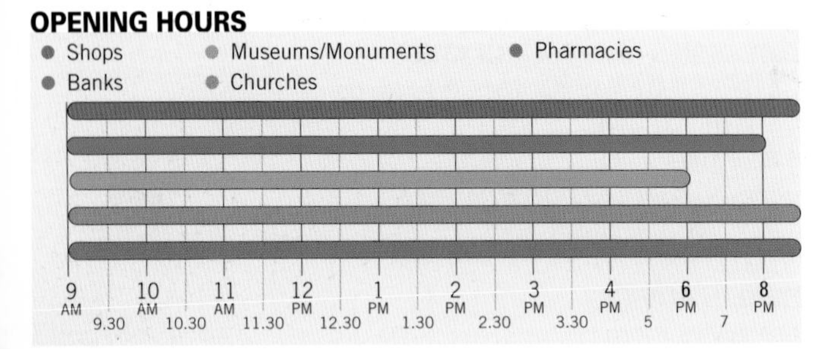

Most shops are closed on Saturday afternoon and all day Sunday. Some shops close for a break on weekday afternoons. Shopping centres in Zagreb, and shops in coastal resorts in summer, may stay open for longer hours and on Sundays. Banks and post offices are generally open on Saturday mornings. Post offices in large cities and popular tourist resorts are open from 7am to 10pm. In larger towns, there will usually be a duty pharmacy open at night, during holidays and at weekends. Museums are generally closed on Mondays and on weekend afternoons.

LANGUAGE

The official language of Croatia is Croatian *(hrvatski)*. Until 1991 this was known as Serbo-Croat but it is now recognized as a separate language. Unlike Serbian, which uses Cyrillic script, Croatian uses the Latin alphabet, otherwise many words are identical. The Croatian language is entirely phonetic, which means that every word is pronounced exactly as it is written. Additional letters used in Croatian are č (pronounced "ch"), ć (almost the same), š (pronounced "sh"), ž (pronounced like a "j") and đ (pronounced "dj"). The letter "c" is pronounced "ts".

hello/good day	*dobar dan*	go away!	*odlazi!*
good morning	*dobro jutro*	yes/no	*da/ne*
good evening	*dobra večer*	here you are	*izvolite*
goodbye	*doviđenj*	cheers!	*¡ivjeli!*
please	*molim*	large	*velik*
thank you	*hvala*	small	*malen*
excuse me	*oprostite*	I don't understand	*ne razumijem*
hotel	*hotel*	telephone	*telefon*
rooms	*sobe*	television	*televizor*
apartment	*apartman*	breakfast	*doručak*
bath/shower	*kupaona/tuš*	half-board	*polupansion*
toilet	*zahod*	key	*ključ*
balcony	*balkon*	reservation	*rezervacija*
bank	*banka*	stamp	*poštanske marka*
exchange	*mjenjacnica*	postcard	*razglednica*
cashier	*blagajnik*	cheap	*jeftino*
money	*novac*	expensive	*skupo*
credit card	*kreditna karta*	open	*otvoreno*
post office	*pošta*	closed	*zatvoreno*
restaurant	*restauracija*	beer	*pivo*
cafe	*kavana*	wine	*vino*
cake shop	*slastičarnica*	coffee	*kava*
lunch	*ručak*	tea	*čaj*
dinner	*večeru*	ice cream	*sladoled*
bread	*kruh*	fish	*riba*
water	*voda*	the bill	*račun*
bus/tram	*autobus/tramvaj*	ticket	*karta*
train	*vlak*	timetable	*vozni red*
bus station	*autobusna stanica*	arrival	*dolazak*
train station	*zeljeznički kolodvor*	departure	*odlazak*
airport	*zračna luka*	entrance/exit	*ulaz/izlaz*
port	*luka*	taxi	*taksi*
ferry	*trajekt*	petrol	*benzin*

Best places to see

1 Dioklecijanova Palača, Split

The ruins of a Roman palace in the heart of a modern city provide a fascinating blend of old and new.

Diocletian (245–c312) was born in Salona (► 102), the son of slaves, but rose to become emperor of Rome. Under his reign Christians were persecuted and many were put to death. It was Diocletian who laid the foundations for the division of the Roman Empire into eastern and western spheres, which later became Catholic and Orthodox – a division which continues to affect Balkan politics today.

Around AD305 Diocletian returned to his native Dalmatia, where he lived out his years in retirement. The palace built for this purpose on the waterfront in Split became the nucleus of the modern city. Not much remains of the original palace, but as you wander around you will stumble across ancient Roman stones and columns incorporated into the houses built within the palace walls.

The best approach is through the Bronze Gate on the harbourfront Riva, which leads straight into the **Podrum** or underground halls. This is the best surviving part of the palace and it gives a good idea of the layout, as the rooms here stood directly beneath the main imperial apartments. A marble and mosaic dining table, believed to have been used by Diocletian, was discovered here in 1998.

The colonnaded central courtyard was known as the peristyle and it continues as a focal point today. To one side is the emperor's mausoleum, now the cathedral (➤ 94); across the square, a narrow lane leads to the Temple of Jupiter, occupied by the baptistery, with a carved 11th-century font at its centre.

19K
Peristil; tel: 021 345606
Podrum
Summer Mon–Sat 9–9, Sun 9–6; winter Mon–Sat 9–2 Inexpensive

2 Gornji Grad, Zagreb

Built on a wooded hillside in the 11th century, the medieval core of Gradec is now an atmospheric district of churches, palaces and cobbled streets.

The oldest part of Zagreb is situated on a hill overlooking the modern city. Although it is possible to walk up, the most enjoyable way of getting there is on the funicular railway, which departs every 10 minutes from

Tomićeva, near Trg Bana Jelačića. This was the first public transport in Zagreb when it opened in 1893. The ascent takes less than a minute and is claimed to be the shortest public transport journey in the world.

Walking ahead past the Lotrščak Tower, you soon reach Markov trg (St Mark's Square), the focal point of the Gornji Grad (Upper Town). The square has an important role as the heart of government in Croatia. On the right is the Sabor (Parliament), where independence was declared in 1991. On the left is the Banski Dvor, the president's official residence which in the same year was hit by a rocket attack that came perilously close to wiping out Croatia's first president Franjo Tudman, which would have changed the future of both Zagreb and Croatia. At the heart of the square is St Mark's Church, whose colourful mosaic roof tiles feature the coats of arms of Croatia, Dalmatia, Slavonia and Zagreb.

You can get a sense of the importance of Catholicism in Croatia at the nearby Kamenita Vrata (Stone Gate), one of the original entrances to the city. When a fire in 1731 destroyed most of the surrounding houses, an image of the Virgin was found unharmed in the rubble. The gate houses a shrine, where pilgrims can usually be found lighting candles and offering prayers to the Virgin.

Zagreb 3f Tram 1, 6, 11, 12, 13, 14, 17 to Trg Bana Jelačića then funicular to Gradec

3 Gradske Zidine, Dubrovnik

A promenade around the city walls offers a magnificent panorama over Dubrovnik, with views across the restored rooftops and out to sea.

There can be no better introduction to Dubrovnik than to walk the 2km (1.25-mile) circuit of its medieval walls. High above the old town, you peer into secret gardens and cloisters that are out of sight at street level. From here you also get a sense of the damage caused during the 1991–92 siege, with gleaming new roof tiles illustrating the fact that over 70 per cent of houses took direct hits.

There was a wall around Dubrovnik in the eighth century, but the present walls date from the 15th-century heyday of the Ragusan republic. Up to 25m (82ft) in height and 6m (20ft) in width, they are reinforced with bastions and towers. Each of the sea-facing bastions, as well as the five gates, is protected by an effigy of St Blaise, Dubrovnik's patron saint.

Access to the ramparts is at three different places, though most people begin a circuit just inside Pile Gate (the others are at Ploče Gate and St John's Fort). Walking clockwise, you first climb to the Minčeta Tower, designed by the Florentine Michelozzo Michelozzi in 1455 and completed by

Juraj Dalmatinac (George the Dalmatian), architect of Šibenik Cathedral. This is literally and metaphorically the high point of the walk, and you can climb to the roof for the best views. Continue in the same direction to pass above the Old Port and return on the seaward side.

The ticket, funds from which are used to support restoration projects, also gives access to Fort Lovrijenac, a free-standing fortress outside Pile Gate.

Dubrovnik 15K Main access from Pile Gate
Summer daily 9–7; winter 9–3 Expensive 1A, 1B, 2, 3, 4, 5, 6, 8, 9

4 Hvar

www.tzhvar.hr

The sunniest island in the Adriatic is an idyllic place of lavender fields and vineyards, whose capital is fast becoming Croatia's glitziest resort.

So confident were Hvar's hoteliers in the island's legendary climate that they used to offer free accommodation in the event of snow – something that happened in 2005 for the first time in 10 years. Here the scent of sage and rosemary hangs in the air, and during the lavender harvest in early summer the countryside is a riot of purple.

The island's capital, Hvar town, has been christened the "new St Tropez" because of the number of celebrities cruising by on their private yachts. Over the last few years Hvar has become the place to be seen on the Adriatic coast and there are now numerous upmarket restaurants and chic boutiques.

The best way to arrive is undoubtedly by boat, sailing into the harbour with its waterfront houses overlooked by a Venetian fortress and medieval walls. The main square fronts directly onto the sea, with a cathedral at one end and the former Venetian arsenal at the

other. The top floor of the arsenal houses one of Europe's oldest public theatres, which opened in 1612 and has recently been restored with two tiers of boxes.

There are beaches just to the west of Hvar Town, but a better option is to take a water taxi to the offshore Pakleni Islands, with their rocky beaches and pinewoods. There are more good beaches at Stari Grad, the island's chief ferry port, and at Jelsa, an attractive holiday resort with views across to the mainland and boats departing in summer for the beaches of Zlatni Rat (➤ 54) on the neighbouring island of Brač.

20L Ferry from Split to Stari Grad or Drvenik to Sućuraj; ferry and catamaran from Split to Hvar town ? Performances of drama and music in summer at Hvar Theatre and in the cloisters of the Franciscan Monastery
i Trg Svetog Stjepana, Hvar town; tel: 021 741059

5 Mljet

This southern Adriatic island is a place of almost mythical beauty, with pinewoods, sandy beaches and lakes at the heart of its national park.

According to legend, Mljet was the home of the beautiful nymph Calypso, who in Homer's *Odyssey* seduced Ulysses and held him prisoner for seven years in her cave on the south coast of the island.

Whatever the truth of the story, Mljet is an island that continues to captivate visitors today.

Most people visit Mljet on day trips, though the island certainly rewards a longer stay and if you spend the night here you will virtually have it to yourself. For a brief visit, the easiest option is the daily catamaran from Dubrovnik, which operates from June to September, or an organized excursion from resorts such as Cavtat, Korčula and Orebić. The cost of an excursion usually includes entrance for the national park.

The boats dock at Polače, a pretty little harbourside village built around the ruins of a Roman villa. From here, a free national park shuttle bus takes you to Veliko Jezero, the larger of two saltwater lakes inside the park. The ticket also includes a boat transfer to St Mary's Island, where an abandoned 12th-century Benedictine monastery stands alone in the middle of the lake. Another option is to follow the path around the lakeshore to Stari Most (Old Bridge) at the confluence of the two lakes. To explore further, you can rent bikes here in summer; it takes about 30 minutes to cycle around Veliko Jezero, passing the monastery on your way to the open sea.

At the other end of the island, Saplunara has one of Croatia's finest sandy beaches.

22L Restaurants (€€) in Polače and Pomena; also by the lakeshore and on St Mary's Island in summer
Nona Ana catamaran from Dubrovnik

Nacionalni Park Mljet

Prištaniste 2 (by the lake) 020 744058; www.np-mljettravel.com Expensive

6 Nacionalni Park Plitvička Jezera

www.np-plitvicka-jezera.hr

The crystalline lakes and waterfalls of the Plitvice Lakes National Park form Croatia's most spectacular natural sight, attracting more than half a million visitors a year.

Even by the standards of Croatia, the Plitvice Lakes are stunning and it is well worth making the effort to get there despite the long journey from the coastal resorts. Most people come in summer, but the lakes have a different appeal throughout the seasons, covered with snow in winter and full of rushing water when the snows melt in springtime.

This was the first national park in Croatia, created in 1949. Bears, wolves and lynx roam in the fir and beech forests, though you are unlikely to see any of them. It would be easy to spend days wandering around the park on the extensive network of footpaths, and it is possible to do this by staying in one of the on-site hotels. Most visitors, however, make do with a single day, enough to get a feel for the

landscape and see the most spectacular sights.

The entrance ticket includes shuttle buses and boat trips, so you can see quite a lot in a few hours. From the main entry point, Ulaz 1, a short path leads to an observation platform with views over Veliki Slap, the largest waterfall, tumbling 70m (230ft) over a cliff. From here you can walk right around and beneath the falls on specially constructed wooden bridges before taking a boat trip across Jezero Kozjak, the largest lake. To explore further, information boards at the entry points suggest various colour-coded itineraries ranging from two to six hours, using a combination of walking, buses and boats.

5E 75km (47 miles) south of Karlovac, signposted from the A1 motorway 053 751015 Summer daily 7am–8pm; spring/autumn 8–6; winter 8–4 Expensive Cafes (€) and restaurants (€€) at park entrances Bus from Zagreb and Split

7 Pula Arena

One of the largest Roman amphitheatres ever to be built has been providing entertainment for the people of Pula for more than 2,000 years.

Pula has grown into one of Croatia's biggest cities, but at its heart are the remains of a Roman town founded in the first century BC. This was an important administrative centre of around 50,000 people, with temples, town walls and a harbour. The most impressive sight by far is the huge, ruined Roman arena, the sixth largest of its kind in the world.

The arena had space for more than 20,000 spectators, who would come here to watch gladiator fights. Constructed out of local Istrian stone, the theatre was built on a slope, with the result that the outer wall has three storeys on its seaward side and two on the landward side. The lower storeys are decorated with arches while the upper level features rectangular openings. The

audience sat in a semicircle in rows of tiered seats, built to take advantage of the natural incline of the hill. In Roman times, the floor of the arena would have been covered in sand and a large awning was stretched across the roof to shield spectators from the sun.

Today the amphitheatre is still used to host concerts by the likes of Elton John, Placido Domingo, Joe Cocker, Jamiroquai and Sting. It is also used as a venue during the annual Pula film festival. During the day, visitors can wander freely around the arena, admiring the scale of it all. The underground passages, which once acted as prisons and cages for wild animals, now house a mildly diverting display of Roman wine jars and olive presses.

✚ 2E ✉ Ulica Flavijevska, Pula ☎ 052 219028 ⌚ May–Sep daily 8am–9pm; Oct–Apr 9–4 🍴 None 🚌 Bus to Pula ✋ Moderate ? Concerts and performances in summer

8 Rovinj

www.tzgrovinj.hr

With Venetian-style houses leaning into the water, fishing boats on the quayside and wooded islands offshore, Rovinj is the gem of the Istrian coast.

Rovinj (Rovigno) is the perfect Croatian town. Densely packed town houses are crowded onto a narrow peninsula, their brightly coloured facades reflected in the sea. Artists sell their work on cobbled streets. On summer evenings, tourists stroll around the harbourside, enjoying the wine bars, restaurants and ice-cream parlours. Yet Rovinj manages to have a life of its own.

Rovinj was built on an island which was linked to the mainland in 1763. From the large open square in front of the harbour, the Balbi Arch leads into the oldest part of town. The arch, built in 1680 and crowned by a Venetian winged lion, features a relief of a Turk's head on the outside and a Venetian inside, a clear message to the Turks to keep out.

A maze of steep, narrow lanes leads up to the church of St Euphemia. Most people walk up Grisia, the main

street of the old town. This is always lively, especially in summer when numerous artists set up here, but the lanes to either side are more atmospheric, with unexpected hidden courtyards and alleys. The church is dedicated to a third-century martyr from Asia Minor whose body washed up in Rovinj five centuries after her death. There are fabulous sunset views from the terrace.

In summer take a boat trip from the harbour to Crveni Otok (Red Island) to swim from its rocky beaches and enjoy views of Rovinj from the water.

2E Bus from Poreč, Pula and Vrsar Open-air art festival on Grisia, second Sun in Aug; feast of St Euphemia, 16 Sep

Obala Pina Budicina 12; tel: 052 811566

Varaždin

This enjoyable town to the north of Zagreb is a relaxing and prosperous place of artists, musicians and the finest baroque architecture in Croatia.

Varaždin was the capital of Croatia from 1756 to 1776 before being destroyed in a fire, started by an unfortunate young man who tripped over a pig while smoking, setting light to a haystack. He was whipped in front of the town hall for his crime. Rebuilt at the end of the 18th century, the result is a beautifully harmonious town of baroque mansions, town houses and churches, whose traffic-free streets and squares make for some delightful strolling.

Varaždin is proud of its heritage and at times it can feel almost like a theme town, when costumed entertainers take to the streets, the city scribe sells calligraphic passports to tourists and the Changing of the Guard takes place outside the town hall, with guardsmen in bearskin hats and military uniforms performing the ceremony to the sound of drums. There are a number of historical events throughout the year, including the Varaždin Baroque Evenings in autumn, when classical concerts are held in the churches and theatres.

The greatest pleasure in Varaždin is simply wandering around the baroque centre, perhaps pausing for a coffee or an ice cream beneath the clock tower in Trg Kralja Tomislava, the main square.

A short walk from here, the mostly 16th-century castle, **Stari Grad,** can be reached by crossing a drawbridge and moat. The castle, set around a beautiful three-tiered courtyard, is home to the town museum, featuring historical displays and a series of themed galleries depicting the changing tastes in furniture from the 16th to 20th centuries.

6A Bus from Zagreb
Train from Zagreb
Changing of the Guard, May–Oct Sat 11am
Ulica Ivana Padovca 3; tel: 042 210987; www.turizam-vzz.hr

Stari Grad

May–Sep Tue–Sun 10–6; Oct–Apr Tue–Fri 10–3, Sat–Sun 10–1 Moderate

10 Zlatni Rat, Brač

The beach that launched a thousand travel posters – a beautiful sand and shingle spit backed by pinewoods and shifting with the tides.

Despite having more than 5,000km (3,100 miles) of coastline, Croatia is not known for its beaches and many visitors are disappointed to find that most beaches are made up of pebbles or rocks rather than sand. One beach, however, appears on every tourist poster as an iconic image of the Adriatic coast and that is Zlatni Rat (Golden Cape, or Horn).

In truth, even this beach is not ideal for sunbathing as it is mostly composed of gravel, but the setting is magnificent. The best way to appreciate it is probably to arrive by boat, or to look down on Zlatni Rat from the summit of Vidova Gora. Set on a triangular sandbar which juts 300m (328yds) into the sea, the beach subtly changes shape with the actions of the wind and tides. The water is shallow and shelves gently into the sea, making it safe for children, and when things get too hot there is plenty of shade to be found in the pinewoods at the centre.

Unless you have your own boat, you get there by following the 2km (1.25-mile) coastal promenade from Bol. Zlatni Rat is an incredibly popular spot in summer, with day trippers arriving from Split and Hvar. If you want to escape the crowds, there are several pebble beaches in the rocky coves to the west, some of which are used by naturists. A cliff-top path from here leads to the village of Murvica, where you can dine at a rustic terrace *konoba* high above the sea with views across the water to Hvar.

20K Bar (€) at Zlatni Rat, restaurants (€€) in Bol and Murvica Ferry from Split to Supetar; excursion boats from Jelsa and fast ferry from Split to Bol in summer

Polat Bolskih Pomoraca, Bol; tel: 021 635638

Best things to do

Places to have lunch by the sea

Doručak Kod Tihane (€€)
Great fish and seafood on a chic harbourside promenade. One of the best in a town renowned for its excellent seafood restaurants.
✉ Obala Sveti Jurja 5, Vis Town ☎ 021 718472

Galija (€€€)
Top-quality Dalmatian cuisine on a terrace beneath the pine trees. Choose from top-notch seafood and perfectly grilled meat dishes.
✉ Vulićevićeva 1, Cavtat ☎ 020 478566; www.galija.hr/restoran

Kapetanova Kuča (€€€)
Fresh oysters on the Pelješac Peninsula. Choose both the shellfish and the fish direct from their tanks in sight of the oyster beds themselves. A favourite with amorous Croatian couples.
✉ Mali Ston ☎ 020 754555; www.ostrea.hr

La Puntuleina (€€€)
Chic wine bar and restaurant with a balcony over the sea. One of the more refined Rovinj options.
✉ Ulica Svetog Križa 38, Rovinj ☎ 052 813186

Le Mandrać (€€€)
New-wave fish and seafood dishes beside the harbour at Volosko. As-good-as-it-gets modern Croatian cooking and well worth the acclaim heaped on it.
✉ Obala Frana Supila 10, Volosko, Opatija
☎ 051 701357; www.lemandrac.com

Lokanda Peskarija (€€)
Good, no-nonsense fish restaurant down by the old harbour in Dubrovnik. Great value.
✉ Na Ponti, Dubrovnik ☎ 020 324750; www.mea-culpa.hr

Morski Konjic (€€)
Great views across the water to the Pelješac Peninsula. Local boy Marco Polo would have approved of the type of Dalmatian treats he supposedly returned home for.
✉ Šetalište Petra Kanavelića, Korčula ☎ 020 711878

Orhan (€€€)
Smart fish restaurant with a harbourside terrace outside Dubrovnik's city walls. Quality fresh white fish.
✉ Od Tabakarije 1, Dubrovnik ☎ 020 411918; www.restaurant-orhan.com

Veli Jože (€€)
Traditional Istrian cuisine by the harbour. Grilled meats and fish excel along with local wines.
✉ Ulica Svetog Križa 3, Rovinj ☎ 052 816337

Viking (€€€)
Fresh fish, oysters and mussels from the Lim Fjord. Superb shellfish as fresh as can be.
✉ Limski Kanal ☎ 052 448223

Top activities

Canoeing and kayaking: Discover the natural beauty of Croatia at a leisurely pace in a canoe or kayak. Huck Finn organizes guided tours on the Kupa, Mreznica, Zrmanja and Trebizat rivers.

Huck Finn

✉ Grada Vukovara 271, 10 000 Zagreb

☎ 01 618 3333; www.huck-finn.hr

Cycling: There are many bicycle routes in Istria (➤ 159–185), through varying terrain and for all abilities. For details visit www.istra.com/zupan/eng/bike.html.

Diving: Scuba-diving schools are located at most resorts. For information visit www.diving.hr.

Rafting: There is rafting on many rivers including in the Cetina Gorge and on the Una river with Huck Finn, for contact details see Canoeing and kayaking, above.

Rock climbing: In the Paklenica National Park.

Paklenica National Park

✚ H17 ✉ Dr Franje Tuđmana 14, Starigrad-Paklenica ☎ 023 369032; www.paklenica.hr

Sailing: Yachts can be chartered all along the coast. For details visit www.saildalmatia.com.

Swimming: From thousands of rock and pebble beaches.

Tennis: Most large hotels have courts.

Walking: In the Biokovo and Velebit mountain ranges just inland from the Dalmatian coast. For information on walking holidays visit www.headwater.com.

Windsurfing: On Brač (➤ 54–55, 96) and the Pelješac Peninsula (➤ 101). For details of courses and board rental visit www.zlatni-bol.com/windsurfing-kitesurf-croatia.htm.

Places to take the children

Aquarium Pula

In an old Hapsburg fortress on the Punta Verudela Peninsula, this aquarium features large seawater tanks filled with Adriatic fish and marine creatures.

✉ Fort Verudela, Pula ☎ 052 381402; www.aquarium.hr 🕐 Apr–Oct daily 9–9; Nov–Mar Sat–Sun 11–5

Aquarium Rovinj

One of Europe's oldest aquariums, with enjoyable displays of starfish, puffer fish, lobsters and sea creatures.

✉ Obala Giordano Paliage 5, Rovinj ☎ 052 804712 🕐 Apr–Oct daily 9–9

Brijuni Islands

Children will enjoy a miniature train ride through the safari park, which contains descendants of the animals presented to the Yugoslav leader Tito by visiting statesmen (➤ 165).

✉ Boat trips from Fažana ☎ 052 525888; www.brijuni.hr

Bunari – Secrets of Šibenik

Šibenik is the unlikely destination for this multimedia experience, in the vaults of the 15th-century wells opposite the cathedral, where, on a self-guided tour, you can explore the city's heritage through interactive displays on themes ranging from shipwrecks to food and drink.

✉ Trg Republike Hrvatske, Šibenik ☎ 098 265924 🕐 May–Oct daily 9–2, 5–11

Dubrovnik Aquarium

Housed on the ground floor of St John's Fort and built into the city walls, this modest aquarium has seawater tanks containing coral, shells, starfish, seahorses, a loggerhead turtle and several varieties of Adriatic grouper.

✉ Tvrđa Sveti Ivana, Dubrovnik ☎ 020 427937; www.imp-du.com
🕐 Summer daily 9–8; winter Mon–Sat 10–1

Hrvatski Prirodoslovni Muzej (Natural History Museum)
Old-fashioned but engaging museum in the upper town of Zagreb, with hundreds of stuffed animals and birds and a basking shark.
✉ Ulica Demetrova 1, Zagreb ☎ 01 485 1700 ⊕ Tue–Fri 10–5, Sat–Sun 10–1

Mini Croatia
This miniature theme park features reproductions of famous buildings from across Croatia.
✉ 2km (1.25 mile) from centre of Rovinj on the road to Pazin ☎ 091 206 8885 ⊕ Apr–Oct daily 10–6

Staro Selo
The ethnographic museum village at Kumrovec (➤ 140) is always a hit with children, especially in summer when there are displays of craftmaking.
✉ Kumrovec, Zagorje ☎ 049 225830 ⊕ Apr–Sep daily 9–7; Oct–Mar 9–4

Trakošćan
As well as exploring the fairytale castle with its battlements and towers (➤ 146), children can enjoy taking a pedal-boat out for a trip on the lake in summer.
✉ Trakošćan ☎ 042 796422; www.trakoscan.hr ⊕ Apr–Sep daily 9–6; Oct–Mar 9–4

Zoo
Brown bears, wolves, elephants, tigers, lions, leopards, crocodiles, chimpanzees, a penguin pool, an aquarium and a reptile house make this a popular day out. Children will also enjoy strolling in Maksimir Park, with its playgrounds and swings.
✉ Maksimirski Perivoj ☎ 01 230 2199; www.zgzoo.com/hr ⊕ Summer daily 9–8; winter 9–5 (ticket office closes one hour earlier)

a walk along the Lungomare

This nostalgic walk follows the Lungomare (Italian for seafront), the popular name for the coastal path connecting Opatija with neighbouring beaches and towns. Begun in 1885 after the opening of the first hotels in Opatija, its full name is Šetalište Franz Josef I, after the Austro-Hungarian emperor of the time.

Start on the seafront in Opatija. The path is straightforward to follow as it clings to the shore in both directions.

The total length of the Lungomare is 12km (7.5 miles), running from Volosko, north of Opatija, down to Lovran, south of Opatija.

The shorter stretch heads north from Opatija, passing the lush gardens of Villa Angiolina and Hotel Kvarner on its way out of town. Continue for around 4km (2.5 miles) to reach the fishing port of Volosko, with several excellent restaurants around the harbour.

Alternatively, you can head south from Opatija for 8km (5 miles) to Lovran. This is a lovely walk past elegant gardens and villas, palm, cypress and chestnut trees, and a rocky shoreline punctuated by

pebble beaches. The promenade is lined with old-fashioned lamps and in places it forms arcades carved into the rock.

Passing the last cafés and ice-cream parlours, you leave Opatija behind. After 3km (2 miles) you reach Ičići, with a marina and beach. The path now continues to Ika, a small village with a terrace restaurant right on the beach.

Eventually, you reach Lovran, with its grand 19th-century villas. If you have the energy retrace your steps to Opatija; if not, there are regular buses.

Distance 8km (5 miles) each way, or 4km (2.5 miles) each way
Time 3 hours
Start point Opatija ✚ 3D
End point Lovran or Volosko
Lunch Ika (€€); on the beach at Ika; tel: 051 291777

Stunning views

Cres: the view over Beli from the Caput Insulae eco-trail (➤ 162).

Dubrovnik: the view over the rooftops from the city walls (➤ 40–41).

Grožnjan: the view out to sea from the terrace of this Istrian hill town (➤ 161).

Hvar: the view of Hvar town from the sea (➤ 42–43).

Krka National Park: the view from the foot of Skradinski Buk waterfalls (➤ 100–101).

Magistrala: magnificent views all along the Dalmatian coast with numerous highlights including the Makarska Rivijera (➤ 98–99) where limestone crags sweep down to the sparkling Adriatic.

Plitvička Jezera: the view across Plitvice Lakes from the *vidikovac* (viewpoint) above the falls (➤ 46–47).

Rovinj: the view from the sea on the boat trip from Crveni Otok (➤ 50–51).

Zadar: sunset from the steps of the Sea Organ (➤ 106–107).

Zagreb: the view over the city from Medvedgrad, a 13th-century fortress in Medvednica Nature Park (➤ 129).

Best summer festivals

Histria Festival

Opera, ballet, orchestral and pop concerts in the Roman arena in July and August.

✉ Pula ☎ 052 522720; www.histriafestival.com

International Folklore Festival

Held in late July, with daily performances of music and dance in the upper town and Trg Bana Jelačića.

✉ Zagreb ☎ 01 450 1194; www.msf.hr

Jeunesses Musicales Croatia
International summer school of young musicians with jazz and classical concerts in July and August.
✉ Grožnjan ☎ 01 611 1600; www.hgm.hr

St Donat's Musical Evenings
International music festival of early music recitals in St Donat's Church in July and August.
✉ Zadar ☎ 023 314552; www.donat-festival.com

Street Art Festival
Held in early August, this festival features performances of dance, theatre, art and acrobatics in the streets and squares of the old part of Poreč.
✉ Poreč ☎ www.street-art-festival.com

Summer Festival
The Libertas summer festival (10 July–25 August) is Croatia's biggest cultural event, with six weeks of open-air music and drama at venues including Fort Lovrijenac and the atrium of the Rector's Palace.
✉ Dubrovnik ☎ 020 326100; www.dubrovnik-festival.hr

Summer Festival
Opera, music and dance throughout the city from mid-July to mid-August, with some performances in the impressive Croatian National Theatre and others in the peristyle courtyard of Diocletian's Palace.
✉ Split ☎ 021 344999; www.splitsko-ljeto.hr

Varaždin Baroque Evenings
Classical concerts in the city's churches, palaces and theatre in late September and early October.
✉ Varaždin ☎ 042 212907; www.vbv.hr

Best national and nature parks

NATIONAL PARKS

The country's first national park was established at the Plitvice Lakes in 1949. Croatia now has eight national parks, all in areas of great scenic beauty, where conservation is taken seriously and tourism strictly controlled. You have to pay a fee to enter these parks.

- Brijuni (➤ 164–165)
- Kornati Islands (➤ 98)
- Krka (➤ 100–101)
- Mljet (➤ 44–45)
- North Velebit: mountainous region overlooking Kvarner bay ✚ D3/4–E4
- Paklenica: limestone gorges in Velebit mountain range near Zadar ✚ F4/5
- Plitvička Jezera (➤ 46–47)
- Risnjak (➤ 172–173)

NATURE PARKS

These are typically situated in areas of population rather than wilderness. Access is generally free.

- Biokovo: table mountain overlooking Makarska Rivijera ✚ K20/21
- Kopački Rit (➤ 138)
- Lastivo Island ✚ M20/21
- Lonjsko Polje (➤ 142–143)
- Medvednica (➤ 129)
- Papuk: mountain in central Slavonia ✚ C9
- Telaščica: northern extension of the Kornati Islands ✚ J17
- Učka: mountain dividing Istria from Rijeka ✚ D2
- Velebit: mountain range overlooking Kvarner bay ✚ D3/4
- Vransko Jezero: Croatia's biggest lake, near Zadar ✚ J17
- Žumberak-Samoborsko Gorje (➤ 145)

Exploring

Each region of Croatia has its own particular appeal. The vast majority of visitors stay on the islands and the coast, which stretches from the Istrian peninsula in the north to Dalmatia in the south.

The World Heritage city of Dubrovnik is situated in southern Dalmatia, but has enough outstanding late-medieval sights to merit a separate chapter of its own. From here, the Magistrala coast road runs north along the Adriatic shore, with ferries linking the mainland to the islands and providing the opportunity for a relaxed island-hopping trip.

The coast may be the highlight of the country, but you have not experienced Croatia until you have seen the inland regions, with the stunning natural scenery of the Plitvice Lakes and the handsome Hapsburg-era cities of Zagreb, Osijek and Varaždin. You need several visits to really get to know this fascinating country.

Dubrovnik and Southern Dalmatia

Dubrovnik stands on a rocky peninsula, surrounded by its medieval walls. For 450 years this was the republic of Ragusa, a powerful maritime city-state that attracted the greatest artists, writers and architects of the time.

Twice in its history, after the earthquake of 1667 and the siege of 1991–92, Dubrovnik has been threatened with extinction, but each time it recovered. Dubrovnik today is a prosperous city, enjoying a second golden age as Croatia's greatest tourist attraction.

✈ 23L

ℹ Stradun, Placa bb; tel: 020 426 354; www.dubrovnik-online.com

DOMINIKANSKI SAMOSTAN (DOMINICAN MONASTERY)

The two great religious institutions of Dubrovnik were built at either end of the old town, inside the Pile and Ploče gates. This 15th-century monastery and cloister managed to survive the earthquake, though the bell tower was added later. Highlights of the museum include an 11th-century Bible manuscript and a painting of Mary Magdalene by Titian, along with the sculpture of the Virgin and Child by Ivan Meštrović in the church.

Dubrovnik 15K Ulica Svetog Dominika 4 020 321 423 Summer daily 9–6; winter 9–5 Inexpensive

FRANJEVAČKI SAMOSTAN (FRANCISCAN MONASTERY)

www.malabraca.hr

Just off the Stradun inside the Pile Gate, the cool cloisters of the Franciscan monastery make a good place to escape the summer heat. The former monastic dispensary founded in 1317 is said to be the oldest continuously operating pharmacy in Europe. The museum contains Serbian shells which struck the monastery in 1991. Also on display is *Novi Prsten* (New Ring), a charming portrait of his wife by local artist Vlaho Bukovac (1855–1922).

Dubrovnik 13L Placa 2 020 321 410 Daily 9–6 Moderate

GRADSKE ZIDINE (CITY WALLS)

Best places to see, ➤ 40–41.

KATEDRALA (CATHEDRAL)

The cathedral was built in 1713 after an earlier church on this site was destroyed in the earthquake. The attraction here is the grisly display of relics in the Treasury behind the altar. Many of them were fashioned by local craftsmen using the gold and silver filigree work for which Ragusa was famous. They include an enamelled gold skull case for the head of St Blaise, and richly jewelled reliquaries for the saint's arm and leg, which are paraded around the city on his feast day (3 February). Also here is a 16th-century silver chest, bizarrely said to contain Jesus' nappy.

Dubrovnik 15M · Pred Dvorom · 020 323 459 · Summer daily 8–8; winter Mon–Sat 8–5, Sun 11–5 · Free (Treasury: inexpensive)

KNEŽEV DVOR (RECTOR'S PALACE)

The Ragusan republic was governed by a Great Council of nobles, who would elect a rector *(knez)* from their number and confine him to this palace throughout his term of office, which lasted just one month. The Gothic-Renaissance palace now functions as the city museum, with portraits and furniture from Ragusa's golden age displayed in the state apartments. Classical concerts are held in the courtyard in summer.

Dubrovnik 15L · Pred Dvorom 1 · 020 321 497 · May–Oct daily 9–6; Nov–Apr Mon–Sat 9–2 · Moderate

STRADUN

For all its magnificent architecture, much of the appeal of Dubrovnik lies in sitting at outdoor cafes soaking up the street life. Nowhere is better for doing this than Stradun, the central promenade of the walled town. Once lined with Gothic palaces, Stradun was rebuilt after the earthquake and this is what gives it such a harmonious feel, its identical three-storey houses with arched doorways and green shutters. So many people have walked this street that the flagstones have been polished to a sheen by passing feet. Stradun runs in a straight line from Vrata od Pile (Pile Gate) to the clock tower on Luža Square. From here, a gate leads to the Gradska Luka (Old Port), once busy with maritime activity but now a pleasure harbour, with a cafe in the former arsenal and boats leaving for Cavtat (➤ 84) and Lokrum (➤ 86).

Dubrovnik 14L

SVETOG VLAHA (CHURCH OF ST BLAISE)

The city's favourite church is dedicated to St Blaise, a third-century Armenian bishop who became Dubrovnik's patron saint after he appeared in a dream to a local priest to warn of a Venetian attack. His image can be seen all over the city, including the sculptures in the niches on the outsides of Pile and Ploče gates. The altar contains a gilded silver statue of St Blaise holding a model of pre-earthquake Dubrovnik.

Dubrovnik 15L Luža 3 Daily 8–7 Free

TVRĐAVA SVETI IVANA (ST JOHN'S FORT)

This 16th-century fortress stands guard over the Old Port. The ground floor houses an aquarium, while the upper floor has been turned into a maritime museum devoted to Dubrovnik's seafaring history, with maps, nautical charts and models of argosies – the merchant ships which took their name from Ragusa.

✝ Dubrovnik 16L ✉ Kneza Damjana Jude 12 ☎ 020 323 978 🕐 Varied opening hours 🖐 Museum: moderate; Aquarium: moderate

a walk in Dubrovnik Old Town

Cars are not allowed inside the old city, making it perfect for walking. Most local buses stop outside Pile Gate, the obvious starting-point for a walk.

Cross the stone bridge and a wooden drawbridge to reach the outer gate, topped by a statue of St Blaise. Pass through the inner gate, also sporting an effigy of the saint, to arrive on Stradun.

To your right is the large Onofrio Fountain, built in 1444.

Walk straight ahead along Stradun and take the first right, passing beneath an archway into Ulica Garište. Turn left at the crossroads into Ulica Od Puča.

This is the main shopping street of the old town, with several art galleries and jewellery shops.

Continue to the end of the street to arrive in Gundulićeva Poljana, scene of a lively morning market.

Keep straight on across the square to emerge in front of the Rector's Palace. Turn left to return to Stradun beneath the clock tower.

The Gradska Kavana cafe makes a good place to take in the atmosphere, with a terrace facing Stradun and St Blaise's Church across the square.

Turn left along Stradun and take the second right onto Ulica Žudioska, at the heart of the old Jewish ghetto. Climb the steps past the synagogue to reach Prijeko.

This busy street, parallel to Stradun, has many tourist-oriented restaurants.

Keep climbing to arrive on Peline, the highest street of the old town. Turn left and follow this lane inside the medieval walls. Just before reaching the Minčeta Tower, turn left along Palmotićeva and take the steep steps downhill to return to Stradun near the Pile Gate.

Distance 1km (0.6 miles)
Time 1 hour
Start/end point Vrata od Pile (Pile Gate) Dubrovnik 13L
1A, 1B, 2, 3, 4, 5, 6, 8, 9
Lunch Kamenice (€€); Poljana Gundulićeva 8; tel: 020 323682

Southern Dalmatia

CAVTAT

Conveniently situated just a few kilometres from the airport, Cavtat is the most attractive of the so-called Dubrovnik Riviera resorts. With regular taxi boats in summer to Dubrovnik's Old Port, it makes the perfect base for anyone looking to combine a beach holiday with a city break. Two sheltered bays are divided by a wooded promontory, with a palm-lined promenade and seafront paths leading to sand and pebble beaches. A path leads to the summit of the peninsula, where the cemetery contains a domed mausoleum designed for a local family by Ivan Meštrović. This was the site of the Greek colony of Epidaurum, one of the first settlements in Croatia in the third century BC, pre-dating Dubrovnik by a thousand years.

Cavtat is the main town of the Konavle region, a fertile strip of farmland which extends to the border with Montenegro. The people of the Konavle are known for their colourful costumes, and folklore performances are held on Sunday mornings in summer in the nearby village of Čilipi.

23M Bus 10 from Dubrovnik Boat from Dubrovnik
Tiha 3; tel: 020 478 025

ELAFITSKI OTOCI (ELAFITI ISLANDS)

The peaceful, traffic-free isles of Koločep, Lopud and Šipan have long provided relaxing retreats for the people of Dubrovnik. There are few permanent residents, but many people have summer homes here and tourism is an important source of income. Besides walking among orchards, gardens and vineyards, the main draws are the easygoing pace of life and the many secluded beaches and coves. The best sandy beach is at Šunj on Lopud. You can visit the islands by ferry from Gruž harbour or by shuttle boats from Dubrovnik's Old Port.

22L Ferry from Dubrovnik
Lopud; tel: 020 759086 (summer only)

LOKRUM

If you only make one trip out of Dubrovnik, it should be to the wooded isle of Lokrum, which is clearly visible just offshore as you walk around the city walls. Boats depart regularly in summer from the Old Port, and the journey takes just 15 minutes. For the people of Dubrovnik, Lokrum is a garden of Eden, a place of legendary beauty where they go to escape the summer heat by strolling through its gardens and relaxing on its beaches. One early visitor was the English king Richard the Lionheart (1157–99), who is said to have been shipwrecked here on his way back from the Crusades and to have built a cathedral in Dubrovnik to give thanks for his survival. Much later, in 1806, the French built a fortress on the summit of the island; you can climb onto the roof for panoramic views.

A short walk from the harbour leads to an abandoned Benedictine monastery, with cloisters and formal gardens. The nearby Mrtvo More (Dead Sea) saltwater lake has good swimming, though many people prefer the island's nudist beach.

23M Boats depart every 30 mins Apr–Oct daily 9–5, weather permitting Boat trip: moderate Café (€) near harbour; restaurant (€€) in monastery in summer Boat from Dubrovnik

TRSTENO ARBORETUM

The gardens at Trsteno are a rare survivor from the days of the Ragusan republic, when statesmen and aristocrats would retire in summer to their Renaissance villas outside the city. Laid out in the 16th century, the gardens make a lovely place to stroll, with shady avenues and an ornamental grotto flanked by statues of nymphs. A path leads down to Trsteno's harbour, with dreamy views of the Elafiti Islands across the water.

23L Trsteno, 24km (15 miles) north of Dubrovnik 020 751019 Summer daily 8–7; winter 8–5 Bus from Dubrovnik Moderate

HOTELS

Grand Villa Argentina (€€€)
Film stars Richard Burton and Elizabeth Taylor, and the Yugoslav leader Tito, all stayed at this smart hotel, with clifftop villas and a private beach and views.
✉ Frana Supila 14 ☎ 020 440555; www.gva.hr

Hilton Imperial (€€€)
With an enviable setting right outside the Pile Gate this elegant hotel seamlessly combines a sense of history (it is one of Dubrovnik's oldest hotels) with the modern conveniences that you might expect from the Hilton group.
✉ Ulica Marijana Blažica 2 ☎ 020 320320; www.hilton.co.uk/dubrovnik

Pucić Palace (€€€)
Luxury town-house hotel in an 18th-century palace on the market square, with dark oak floors, antique furniture, modern art and a private yacht for guests.
✉ Ulica Od Puča 1 ☎ 020 326200; www.thepucicpalace.com

Stari Grad (€€€)
One of only two hotels within the medieval walls, this has eight rooms in an old town house close to Pile Gate. The rooftop terrace has views over the city.
✉ Od Sigurate 4 ☎ 020 322244; www.hotelstarigrad.com

Villa Dubrovnik (€€€)
Romantic seaside villa set among orange trees, with its own beach and shuttle boats to the old town.
✉ Ulica Vlaha Bukovca 6 ☎ 020 422933; www.villa-dubrovnik.hr
🕐 Closed Dec–Feb

RESTAURANTS

Antunini (€€)
With its plush red curtains, gilded mirrors and chandeliers, this restaurant recreates the feel of Ragusa's medieval guilds.
✉ Prijeko 30 ☎ 020 321199 🕐 Daily 9am–midnight

Buffet Škola (€)
The thick crusty sandwiches here are the best in town, stuffed full of Dalmatian cheese and ham. Found on an alley off the Stradun, with steps leading up to Prijeko.
✉ Antuninska 1 ☎ 020 321096 🕐 Daily 9am–10pm

Café Festival (€)
This popular cafe is the best place for people-watching on the Stradun. Good coffee, cakes and Italian bruschetta.
✉ Stradun 1 ☎ 020 321148 🕐 Daily 8am–2am

Kamenice (€€)
The name means "oyster" and this busy lunchtime bar on the market square serves a simple but delicious menu of seafood, fried fish, risotto and salads.
✉ Poljana Gundulićeva 8 ☎ 020 323682 🕐 Daily 8am–11pm

Lokanda Peskarija (€€)
Popular open-air fish restaurant right by the Old Port, serving mussels, prawns, squid, grilled fish and seafood risotto.
✉ Na Ponti ☎ 020 324750; www.mea-culpa.hr 🕐 Daily 11am–11pm

Mea Culpa (€)
Bustling pizzeria in the back lanes of the old town, with tables out of doors on a cobbled street.
✉ Za Rokom 3 ☎ 020 323430; www.mea-culpa.hr 🕐 Daily 8am–midnight

Nautika (€€€)
Top-notch fish and seafood in the old nautical academy outside Pile Gate, with two floors of dining plus a seafront summer terrace.
✉ Brsalje 3 ☎ 020 442526; www.esculap-teo.hr 🕐 Daily 12–12

Orhan (€€€)
Charming and romantic fish restaurant overlooking a small cove beach beneath Fort Lovrijenac, with a seaside terrace.
✉ Od Tabakarije 1 ☎ 020 411918; www.restaurant-orhan.com 🕐 Daily 11am–midnight

Rozarij (€€)
On a busy street of tourist restaurants, this one stands out for its cozy atmosphere and authentic Dalmatian cuisine, such as black cuttlefish risotto.
✉ Zlatarska 4 ☎ 020 322 015 🕐 Daily 11am–midnight

SHOPPING

Dubrovačka Kuća
Small shop and art gallery near the Dominican monastery selling a wide range of Dalmatian and Croatian wines, liqueurs, natural cosmetics and crafts.
✉ Ulica Svetog Dominika ☎ 020 322092

Medusa
If you're after good quality souvenirs then this is the place to start. Medusa offers a good selection of contemporary and traditional handicrafts as well as Croatian spirits.
✉ Prijeko 18 ☎ 020 322004; www.medusa.hr

Vinoteka Dubrovnik
Visit this well-stocked wine shop to pick up a bottle or two of Croatian wine. Impress your friends back home with a full-bodied Dingac or a refreshing Malvazija.
✚ Pred Dvorom 1 ☎ 020 321202; www.mea-culpa.hr

ENTERTAINMENT

Buža
Dubrovnik's most atmospheric bar, in a spectacular position on a palm-shaded waterfront terrace, perched on the rocks outside the city walls. Get there by following the sign saying "Cold Drinks" through a gap in the walls and down the steps.
✉ Access from Ulica Od Margarite ☎ No phone 🕐 Open in good weather

Troubadour
Jazz cafe near the cathedral, with live music on an outdoor terrace at 10pm nightly in summer.
✉ Bunićeva Poljana 2 ☎ 020 323476 🕐 Daily 10am–2am

Split and Dalmatia

From pine-fringed islands surrounded by turquoise seas to pretty little fishing ports and historic Venetian towns, Dalmatia has it all. Travelling around the region is easy on the Magistrala coastal highway, or you can go island-hopping using the excellent network of ferries. The islands of Brač, Hvar and Korčula are justifiably popular but it is worth making the effort to seek out some of the more remote islands such as Vis and the Kornati archipelago.

Although most travellers head for the islands, the major cities of northern and central Dalmatia also reward exploration. Split and Zadar have Roman remains and a vibrant cafe life, while Šibenik makes a good base for excursions into the Krka National Park. Other highlights are the World Heritage town of Trogir, the beaches of the Makarksa riviera, and the mountainous Pelješac peninsula, which produces some of Croatia's finest and most expensive red wines.

SPLIT

Croatia's second city is the source of much regional pride, enjoying a fierce rivalry with Zagreb in everything from fashion to football. This is a modern port city and the hub of the Dalmatian ferry network with boats leaving for many islands including Brač, Hvar, Korčula and Vis. Street life centres on the waterfront Riva, crowded with open-air cafes. The main sights are around Diocletian's Palace (➤ 36–37) and on the Marjan Peninsula to the west.

www.visitsplit.com

19K

Peristil bb; tel: 021 345 606

Arheološki Muzej (Archaeological Museum)

Croatia's oldest museum, founded in 1820, features objects excavated from the Roman city at Salona (➤ 102). Among the items on display are jewellery, pottery, glass jars, coins and a second-century mosaic of the god Apollo. Also here are ancient Greek artefacts from the island of Vis, including wine jars and a beautiful clay oil lamp depicting the gods Isis and Serapis. The semi-circular courtyard gallery contains examples of Roman art, with mosaics and sarcophagi featuring scenes of everyday life such as chariot racing, hunting and bunches of grapes.

Zrinsko-Frankopanska 25 021 329340; www.mdc.hr Mon–Sat 9–2, 4–8 Moderate

Dioklecijanova Palača (Diocletian's Palace)

Best places to see, ➤ 36–37.

Etnografski Muzej (Ethnographic Museum)

Housed inside the vestibule of Diocletian's palace, this enjoyable museum features traditional folk costumes from both coastal and inland Dalmatia. Among the displays are cavalry uniforms, fur hats, swords and lances from the Sinjska Alka, an annual festival of jousting and horsemanship held in the nearby town of Sinj each August to commemorate a victory over the Ottoman Turks in 1715.

Ulica Severova 1 021 344161 Summer Mon–Fri 9–9, Sat 9–1, Sun 10–1; winter Mon–Fri 9–2, Sat 9–1 Inexpensive

Galerija Meštrović

The sculptor Ivan Meštrović (1883–1962) spent much of his childhood in Dalmatia and he planned this grand villa as his summerhouse and studio, though he only lived here for two years before spending the rest of his life in exile in the United States. The house and garden contain a representative collection of his work, including female nudes, family portraits and religious studies. The ticket also includes entry to the nearby Kaštelet, a 16th-century chapel bought by Meštrović to house his *Life of Christ* cycle.

✉ Šetalište Ivana Meštrovića 46 ☎ 021 340800; www.mdc.hr 🕐 May–Sep Tue–Sun 9–7; Oct–Apr Tue–Sat 9–4, Sun 10–3 🚌 Bus 12 Moderate

Katedrala (Cathedral)

Situated in the central peristyle court of Diocletian's palace and guarded by a black granite sphinx from Egypt, the octagonal temple designed

as the emperor's mausoleum was later turned into the city's cathedral. Look carefully into the dome and you can still make out reliefs of chariot races from Roman times, together with portraits of Diocletian and his wife. The cathedral is full of symbolism – the pulpit was carved out of stone from Diocletian's tomb and there are altars to two bishops martyred by Diocletian. You can climb the separate bell-tower for views over the city.

✉ Peristil 🕐 Summer daily 8–8; winter Mon–Sat 8–12, 4–7
💰 Inexpensive

Marjan

Climb the steps on Senjska at the west end of the Riva to reach the Marjan Peninsula, a cool green hill overlooking the city. This is where people come to escape the summer heat, with shady woodland walks, ancient hermitage chapels and peaceful views out to sea. The cafe terrace at the top of the steps is a popular lookout point. A path from here leads to the summit.

🍴 Caffe Vidilica (€)

Dalmatia

BRAČ

The best-known attraction on Brač may be the beach at Zlatni Rat (➤ 54–55), but there is more to the island than that. This is the largest island off the Dalmatian coast, watched over by Vidova Gora, at 778m (2,544ft) the highest peak on any Croatian island. Brač is famous for its white marble stone, quarried here since Roman times and used in buildings ranging from Diocletian's palace in Split (➤ 36–37) to Liverpool Cathedral in the UK and the White House in Washington DC. Ferries from Split arrive at Supetar, a sleepy town set around a harbour. Milna, on the west coast, is another attractive village in a sheltered bay.

20K Ferry from Split or Makarska

Porat Bolskih Pomoraca, Bol; tel: 021 635638; www.bol.hr

HVAR

Best places to see, ➤ 42–43.

KORČULA

Crowded onto a narrow peninsula with the sea on three sides and enclosed by medieval walls, Korčula resembles a smaller version of Dubrovnik. The entry to the old town is through the 15th-century Land Gate, where a broad flight of steps leads up to an archway crowned by a winged lion, the symbol of Venice. From here, you plunge into a maze of narrow lanes with a cathedral at the centre and a promenade leading around the outer walls.

Korčula claims to be the birthplace of the explorer Marco Polo (1254–1324), who was captured here in 1298. The island is also famous for the Moreška sword dance, a good-versus-evil tale of

Moors and Christians which arrived in the 16th century and is still performed on summer evenings. Just outside Korčula, the village of Lumbarda has vineyards and a sandy beach.

20L Bus from Dubrovnik Ferry from Dubrovnik or Orebić

Obala Vinka Paletina; tel: 020 715 867

KORNATI OTOCI (KORNATI ISLANDS)

This archipelago of more than 100 rocky islands, including Kornati and Murter, off the north Dalmatian coast is a paradise for sailors, with calm seas, crystal-clear waters and a remote, ethereal beauty. The Irish playwright George Bernard Shaw (1856–1950) wrote that when the gods wanted to crown their work, on the last day they created Kornati "from their tears, the stars and their breath".

For much of the year the islands are uninhabited but in summer the residents of Murter, owners of most of the land, set up fish restaurants for visiting yachtsmen and rent out old fishermen's cottages for a "Robinson Crusoe" experience, with no electricity, water from a well and supplies delivered by boat. For a shorter visit, travel agents in Murter, Zadar and Šibenik offer regular full-day excursions in summer.

17J Boat trips from Murter, Zadar and Šibenik

Nacionalni Park Kornati

Ulica Butina 2, Murter; tel: 022 435740; www.np-kornati.htnet.hr

Expensive (included in cost of boat excursion)

MAKARSKA RIVIJERA

From Brela in the north to Gradac in the south, the Makarska riviera is a 60km (37-mile) stretch of coastal resorts linked by the Magistrala highway. The coastline has been subjected to intense tourism development, and the towns along this strip lack the history and character of places such as Dubrovnik and Korčula. Nevertheless, former fishing villages like Brela and Baška Voda retain a fair amount of charm, and there are some excellent white-pebble beaches at Brela, Makarska, Tučepi and Gradac. Makarska itself is a pleasant harbourside town, with ferries leaving for Brač and a palm-lined promenade leading around a horseshoe bay. The coastline is overlooked by the Biokovo table mountain (1,762m/5,762ft), the second highest in Croatia.

20K Bus from Split and Dubrovnik

Obala Kralja Tomislava, Makarska; tel: 021 612002; www.makarska.hr

MLJET

Best places to see, ➤ 44–45.

NACIONALNI PARK KRKA

The gorges and waterfalls of the River Krka rival the Plitvice Lakes (➤ 46–47) for their beauty, and are much easier to visit if you are staying on the Dalmatian coast. The highlight is Skradinski Buk, a 45m (148ft) series of cascades tumbling into a pool where people go swimming in summer. From the top of the waterfall, boat trips make the journey along a wooded canyon to the islet of Visovac,

home to a Franciscan monastery founded in 1445. Some of the trips continue to a second waterfall at Roški Slap. Even without the boat trip, it is worth visiting the park to walk around the waterfall at Skradinski Buk. You can get there by national park boat from the village of Skradin, or shuttle bus from Lozovac.

www.npkrka.hr

18J 12km (7 miles) north of Šibenik 022 201777 Summer daily 8–8; winter 9–4 Cafes (€) at Skradinski Buk and Roški Slap Bus from Šibenik Expensive

PELJEŠAC

The Pelješac Peninsula is connected to the mainland by a narrow isthmus at Ston. The village of Mali Ston is known for its oysters, while the twin town of Veli Ston is still enclosed by its 14th-century walls. A 90km (56-mile) road crosses the peninsula, climbing high above the coast with views to Korčula, Mljet and Vis. The road passes through the Potomje vineyards, famous throughout Croatia for Dingač, the country's most expensive red wine. In 2007, construction began on a bridge between Pelješac and the mainland, which will unite southern Dalmatia with the rest of Croatia and allow traffic to travel between Dubrovnik and Zagreb without passing through Bosnia-Herzegovina. The project has been affected by economic cuts and is unlikely to open before 2015 at the earliest.

21L Bus from Dubrovnik and Korčula

Ferry from Korčula to Orebić

Trg Mimbeli, Orebić; tel: 020 713718; www.orebic.hr

SALONA

Two thousand years ago, when Split was no more than a fishing village, Salona was the richest city on the coast, a thriving town of 60,000 people and the birthplace of the Roman emperor

Diocletian. The city has long been abandoned, but you can get some sense of its scope by wandering around the ruins. Half-hidden among the fields is the Roman amphitheatre, where gladiatorial contests were held in front of a crowd of 15,000 spectators. Domnius, the first bishop of Salona, was executed in the amphitheatre in AD304 and his tomb can be seen in the ruins of a basilica. There is a small archaeological museum on site, but most of the finds from Salona are in the Archaeological Museum at Split (➤ 93).

19K 5km (3 miles) from Split 021 211538 Summer daily 9–7; winter Mon–Fri 9–3, Sat 9–2 Cafe (€) Bus from Split Moderate

ŠIBENIK

Šibenik stands in a sheltered harbour at the mouth of the River Krka. Although it is now a sprawling industrial city, like so many towns on this coast it has a compact old town at its core. The biggest draw is the cathedral, designed by Juraj Dalmatinac (George the Dalmatian, c1400–73), whose statue, by Ivan Meštrović, stands outside. This is probably the finest example of Venetian Gothic architecture in Croatia, full of delicately carved stonework both inside and out. The frieze of 74 stone heads running around the exterior of the apses are thought to be unflattering portraits of local citizens who refused to pay towards the cost of the building.

www.sibenik-tourism.hr

18J Bus from Split, Trogir and Zadar

Obala Dr Franje Tuđmana 5; tel: 022 214448

TROGIR

Built on a small island and connected by bridges to the mainland and the larger island of Čiovo, Trogir is one of the most attractive towns on the Adriatic coast. It is possible to walk right around the island in under half an hour, but you could easily spend all day getting lost in its narrow streets. The main sight is the cathedral, begun in the 13th century but topped by a distinctive three-storey Venetian campanile, which was completed three centuries later.

The most remarkable feature is the west portal, carved in 1240 and richly illustrated with depictions of everyday farming life including the grape harvest and the annual pig slaughter, together with more conventional angels, saints and scenes from the life of Christ. Inside the cathedral, the greatest

treasure is the 15th-century vaulted chapel of St John.

Across the square is the Venetian loggia, also dating from the 15th century. Much of the action takes place on the Riva, the waterfront promenade, with its numerous cafes and bars. At the west end of the Riva, the Kamerlengo fortress was built as the residence of the Venetian governor; you can stroll around the battlements for views over the town.

www.trogir.hr

19K Bus 37 from Split

Trg Ivana Pavla II; tel: 021 881412

VIS

This remote Adriatic island was first settled by the ancient Greeks, who founded the town of Issa in the fourth century BC. Until 1989, however, Vis was off limits to foreign tourists due to its strategic military importance. During World War II Tito established his base on the island in a cave on Mount Hum, where he held secret meetings with British diplomats and spies. The British connection with Vis goes back much further; the island was occupied by British troops during the Napoleonic wars (1811–15) and it still has a cricket club today. A path on the west side of the harbour climbs to the ruined George III fortress, with a carved Union Jack (British flag) above the door. Across the bay is a small English cemetery, with memorials to the dead of the 19th century and "Tito's liberation war".

Today, Vis is a laid-back island of vineyards and fishing ports, popular with visiting sailors. It has developed an increasingly chic reputation, and there are several expensive fish restaurants by the harbours in both Vis town and Komiža. In summer you can take a boat trip from Komiža to the neighbouring island of Biševo, entering a natural grotto known as the Modra Špilja (Blue Cave).

www.tz-vis.hr

19L Ferry from Split

Šetalište Stare Isse 5; tel: 021 717017

ZADAR

The major city of northern Dalmatia is built on a peninsula, still partly enclosed by its medieval walls. At the heart of it all is the old Roman forum, the stone from which was used to build St Donat's

Church, a ninth-century Byzantine round church dedicated to an Irish bishop. The forum also contains an Archaeological Museum and an exhibition of medieval gold and silver jewellery in the convent of St Mary's Church. Near here is the Morske Orgulje (Sea Organ), built in 2005, where you sit on stone steps on the Riva promenade listening to music created by underwater pipes. Some 20km (12.5 miles) north of Zadar, the island village of Nin was once Croatia's ecclesiastical capital and it contains one of the country's greatest treasures, the tiny, whitewashed 9th-century chapel known as the Cathedral of the Holy Cross.

17J Bus from Šibenik and Split Ferry from Rijeka, Split and Dubrovnik

Ilije Smiljanica 5; tel: 023 316166

ZLATNI RAT, BRAČ

Best places to see, ➤ 54–55

a drive through Northern Dalmatia

This long drive takes you through the Krajina, the historic border region occupied by Serbs living in Croatia. During the war of 1991–95, rebel Serbs declared the Republic of the Serbian Krajina at Knin. After the war, most of the Serbs fled into Bosnia, leaving many villages abandoned. The scars of war are still visible in the ruins of bombed-out houses.

Follow the coast road south for 70km (43 miles) from Zadar to Šibenik, with the mountains on your left and the islands of the Zadar and Kornati archipelagos to your right. On the outskirts of Šibenik, after crossing the

bridge over the River Krka, turn left towards Drniš. Pass the turn-off for the Krka National Park and continue ahead with the Dinaric Mountains on the horizon.

The road climbs to the head of a gorge where you will see the ruined castle above Drniš.

Turn right at Drniš and follow the railway line to Knin.

The town is dominated by its fortress, previously in rebel hands, now symbolically flying the Croatian flag.

Drive through Knin and turn left at the roundabout towards Zagreb. The road climbs onto a plateau. After 7km (4 miles), turn left towards Benkovac. In the village of Kistanje, turn right, signposted to Obrovac. Keep right when the road forks and stay on this road across a bleak landscape of deserted villages.

When you reach a junction, Obrovac is hidden in the gorge to your right, on the Zrmanja river.

Turn left here and stay on this long straight road to return to Zadar.

Distance 230km (143 miles)
Time 5 hours
Start/end point Zadar 17J
Lunch Ankora (€€); Tvrđava (inside the fortress at Knin); tel: 022 663 045

HOTELS

BRAČ

Kaštil (€€)

This small seafront hotel has 32 rooms in a traditional stone building by the harbour. Zlatni Rat is a 2km (1.25 mile) stroll away.
✉ Ulica Frane Radića 1, Bol ☎ 021 635995; www.kastil.hr 🕐 Mar–Oct

Palača Dešković (€€€)

A 15th-century palace converted by Countess Dešković into a stylish hotel, decorated with her own paintings and antiques. It is situated beside the harbour in the pretty village of Pučišća, with private moorings for guests.
✉ Pučišća, Brač ☎ 021 778240; www.palaca-deskovic.com

HVAR

Palace (€€€)

The grande dame of Hvar is set in the old Venetian governor's palace, with views across the harbour from the terrace. Elegant rooms, an outdoor pool and a terrace restaurant are highlights.
✉ Trg Svetog Stjepana, Hvar Town ☎ 021 741966; www.suncanihvar.com

Riva (€€€)

This 100-year-old stone building on the promenade has been converted into the funkiest hotel in town, with cool cocktail bars, contemporary decor and an atmosphere of informal luxury.
✉ Riva, Hvar Town ☎ 021 750 750; www.suncanihvar.com

KORČULA

Korčula (€€)

Family-run hotel on the seaside at Gradac, with a good restaurant, fitness centre and fine views from the rooftop terrace.
✉ Obala Franje Tuđmana 5 ☎ 020 711078; www.korcula-hotels.com

Marko Polo (€€)

Old-fashioned hotel on the waterfront, near the entrance to the old town, with 20 comfortable rooms and a seaside terrace.
✉ Korčula ☎ 020 726100; www.korcula-hotels.com

KORNATI OTOCI

Marina Hramina (€€)

You don't need a yacht to stay here as there are also a few rooms, decked out in nautical style with balconies overlooking the marina.

✉ Put Gradine, Murter ☎ 022 434411; www.marina-hramina.hr

MLJET

Odisej (€€)

The only hotel in the national park looks down over a small cove in Pomena. Walking, cycling and sailing are popular activities here.

✉ Pomena ☎ 020 362111; www.hotelodisej.hr 🕒 Apr–Oct

NACIONALNI PARK KRKA

Skradinski Buk (€)

Small, attractive family-run hotel in the harbourside village of Skradin, near the entrance to the national park.

✉ Burinovac, Skradin ☎ 022 771771; www.skradinskibuk.hr

SPLIT

Peristil (€€)

This modern hotel is built into the walls of Diocletian's Palace. Just 12 rooms and plenty of character in the heart of the city. Regional Dalmatian cuisine is served in the restaurant.

✉ Poljana Kraljice Jelene 5 ☎ 021 329070; www.hotelperistil.com

Vestibul Palace (€€€)

An intriguing blend of ancient and modern, this trendy design hotel is in the vestibule of Diocletian's Palace. Bedrooms and split-level suites available.

✉ Iza Vestibula 4 ☎ 021 329329; www.vestibulpalace.com

TROGIR

Concordia (€€)

Rooms in an 18th-century town house on the Riva, with views across the marina from the seafront terrace.

✉ Obala Bana Berislavića 22 ☎ 021 885400; www.concordia-hotel.net

Pasike (€€)
Small family-run hotel with 14 rooms and and its own restaurant in an old town house decorated throughout with 19th- and 20th-century furniture.
✉ Sinjska ☎ 021 885185; www.hotelpasike.com

VIS

Tamaris (€€)
Many people arrive in Vis on their own yacht but if not, stay in this Hapsburg villa by the harbour, with views across the bay from its spacious, shuttered rooms.
✉ Obala Sveti Jurja 30, Vis town ☎ 021 711350; www.hotelvis.com

ZADAR

Club Funimation Borik (€€€)
Large, all-inclusive beach resort owned by the Austrian Falkensteiner chain, with children's club, indoor and outdoor pools, spa centre and waterpark.
✉ Majstora Radovana 7 ☎ 023 206636; www.falkensteiner.com

RESTAURANTS

BRAČ

Konoba Marija (€€)
A 4km (2.5-mile) clifftop path from Zlatni Rat beach leads to this stunningly situated *konoba* (traditional tavern), with meat and fish cooked on an open grill on a shady terrace high above the sea.
✉ Murvica, Bol ☎ No phone 🕒 Jun–Oct daily 10am–midnight

Palute (€)
Harbourside restaurant offering grilled meat and fish dishes on a seafront terrace, beside the port where ferries arrive from Split.
✉ Porat 4, Supetar ☎ 021 631730 🕒 Daily 10am–midnight

Vladmir Nazur (€€)
This small *konoba* on the summit of Vidova Gora offers a simple menu of ham, cheese and roast lamb, with stunning views.
✉ Vidova Gora ☎ 021 549061 🕒 Daily 10am–midnight in summer

HVAR

Bounty (€€)

Grilled meats, pasta, salad and seafood in a perfect setting beside the inner harbour. The grilled fish and seafood risotto are popular.
☒ Mandrac, Hvar Town ☎ 021 742565 ⌚ Daily 11am–midnight

Konoba Menego (€€)

Simple local produce, such as goat's cheese with honey or figs in brandy, in an old stone house on the castle steps.
☒ Groda, Hvar Town ☎ 021 742036; www.menego.hr ⌚ Apr–Oct daily 12–2, 5–1

Luna (€€)

Fashionable, offbeat bistro and roof garden with Italian-influenced cuisine, such as fresh pasta, steak with truffles and fish casserole.
☒ Ulica Petra Hektorovića 5, Hvar Town ☎ 021 741400 ⌚ Apr–Oct daily 12–12

Paladini (€€€)

Fresh fish and authentic Dalmatian cuisine served in a 16th-century palace overlooking the main square, or in a garden of orange and lemon trees in summer.
☒ Ulica Petra Hektorovića 4, Hvar Town ☎ 021 742104 ⌚ May–Dec daily 12–3, 6–12

Tony (€–€€)

Down-to-earth harbourside bar where fishermen come for breakfast after a morning's catch – just the place for a snack while waiting for your ferry.
☒ Sućuraj ☎ 091 591 3438 ⌚ Daily 6am–midnight

Zlatna Školjka (€€€)

Chic restaurant, in a 13th-century building, specializing in "slow food," with creative variations on local dishes such as gnocchi with almonds and rabbit with figs.
☒ Ulica Petra Hektorovića 8, Hvar Town ☎ 098 168 8797; www.zlatna.skoljka.com ⌚ Apr–Oct daily 12–3, 7–12

KORČULA

Adio Mare (€€)

Bustling *konoba* in the old town, with communal wooden benches and fishing nets draped on the walls. Classic Dalmatian dishes like fish soup and veal stew feature here, alongside meat and fish cooked on an open grill. Adio Mare is popular with both locals and tourists so if you want to dine here at night you should always reserve a table.

✉ Ulica Svetog Roka 2, Korčula Town ☎ 020 711253 ⊙ Apr–Oct daily 6pm–midnight

Maslina (€)

Family-run restaurant on the road from Korčula to Lumbarda. The speciality is *pogača*, like Italian focaccia bread topped with cheese, olives and vegetables.

✉ Lumbarajska Cesta ☎ 020 711720 ⊙ Summer daily 11am–midnight; winter 11–3, 5–midnight

Morski Konjic (€€)

Romantic setting on the sea walls, with tables just above the water. Fresh fish is expensive but there are simpler choices such as salads and grilled meat.

✉ Šetalište Petra Kanavelića, Korčula Town ☎ 020 711878 ⊙ May–Oct daily 8am–midnight

MLJET

Mali Raj (€€)

The name means "little paradise" and the setting on the shores of Veliko Jezero lake is heavenly. Typical Dalmatian cuisine, including grilled meat and fish.

✉ Babine Kuće ☎ 020 744115 ⊙ May–Sep daily 10am–midnight

MURTER

Mate (€€€)

This busy fish restaurant is based around a courtyard north from the harbour. Specialities are grilled fish and *brodet* (fish stew).

✉ Ulica Kornatska 1 ☎ 022 435351 ⊙ Apr–Sep daily 12–12

Tic-Tac (€€)
Buzzy, fashionable bistro in a quiet street near the harbour. Fresh fish dishes, grilled vegetables and octopus sushi.
✉ Ulica Hrokešina 5 ☎ 098 278494 🕐 Apr–Sep daily 12–12,

NACIONALNI PARK KRKA

Kristijan (€)
In an old stone mill above the jetty, this serves simple plates of cured ham and cheese with bread, olives and wine.
✉ Roški Slap ☎ No phone 🕐 Apr–Oct daily lunch only

PELJEŠAC

Kapetanova Kuća (€€€)
Mali Ston is famous for its oysters and this is the best place to try them. Also mussels, lobster and fish.
✉ Mali Ston ☎ 020 754555; www.ostrea.hr 🕐 Daily 9am–midnight

ŠIBENIK

Gradska Vijećnica (€€)
Dalmatian cuisine served amid the splendour of the Venetian Gothic town hall, or on a terrace under the loggia with views across the cathedral square in summer.
✉ Trg Republike Hrvatske 3 ☎ 022 213605 🕐 Daily 8am–midnight

SPLIT

Antika (€€)
This atmospheric cellar wine bar and restaurant is a wonderful place for a romantic meal, or to enjoy fine Croatian by the glass and regional tapas dishes.
✉ Prilaz brace Kaliterna 6 ☎ 099 8073930; www.restoran-antika.com
🕐 Daily 10am–11pm

Hvaranin (€)
Modest *konoba* in the Varoš district, just back from the Riva, offering Dalmatian and Hvar island classics such as stuffed peppers, fried anchovies and boiled lamb.
✉ Ulica Ban Mladenova 9 ☎ 091 767 5891 🕐 Daily 12–4, 6–midnight

Kod Joze (€€)
Traditional cellar restaurant serving fresh fish, steaks, risottos and grilled vegetables in an old stone house or on the terrace, in a quiet lane outside the centre.
Sredmanuška 4 021 347397 Mon–Fri 9am–midnight, Sat–Sun 12–12

Varoš (€€)
This tavern in the Varoš district has fishing nets on the walls and serves fresh fish as well as veal, lamb and octopus cooked under the *peka* (metal lid).
Ulica Ban Mladenova 7 021 396138 Daily 9am–midnight

TROGIR

Fontana (€€)
An expansive waterfront terrace and simply grilled seafood make dining alfresco at Fontana popular with locals and tourists alike.
Obrov 1 021 884 811; www.fontana-trogir.com

Mirkec (€)
Occupying a prime position on the waterfront, this pizzeria makes a good lunchtime spot, with salads, pasta dishes and pizzas.
Budislavićeva 15 021 883042 Daily 10am–midnight

VIS

Bako (€€)
Small fish restaurant right by the water's edge, offering anchovies, sardines, lobster and fresh fish on a vine-covered terrace.
Gundulićeva 1, Komiža 021 713742 Summer daily 11am–2am; winter 5pm–midnight

Jastožera (€€€)
Chic sailors' hangout in Komiža's old lobster-pot house, with wooden platforms above the water and magical sea views. Expensive fish and lobster.
Gundulićeva 6, Komiža 021 713859; www.jastozera.com Summer daily 5pm–2am

Vatrica (€€)

Traditional *konoba* in the village of Kut, specializing in barbecued fish and spaghetti with lobster. Wooden tables on the waterfront, a short walk from Vis town.

✉ Obala Kralja Krešimira 15, Kut ☎ 021 711574 🕐 Summer daily 9am–2am; winter 5–11pm

Villa Kaliopa (€€)

Outdoor tables interspersed with leafy trees and the opportunity to select your own fish from the daily catch combine to make this one of Hvar's most romantic dining options. The former 16th-century palace that houses the restaurant is impressive, but the romance of the garden is hard to beat.

✉ Ulica Vladimira Nazora 32, Vis town ☎ 021 711755 🕐 Summer daily 5pm–midnight in summer

ZADAR

Arsenal (€€)

Lounge bar and restaurant right by the water's edge, offering anchovies, sardines, lobster and a selection of fresh fish on a pretty vine-covered terrace.

✉ Trg Tri Bunara 1 ☎ 023 253833 🕐 Daily 7am–3am

SHOPPING

Galerija Tanja Ćurin

Hvar Town is dotted with jewellery boutiques, but with striking contemporary designs that incorporate fresh water pearls, corals, silver and semi-precious stones this is one of the best.

✚ Matije Ivanića 4, Hvar ☎ 021 742 218; www.tanjacurinjewellery.com.hr

Podrum

The underground cellars of Diocletian's Palace may be unashamedly geared towards tourists, but this makes them a good place to pick up local handicrafts, paintings and other artistic souvenirs.

✚ Underground chambers situated between the Peristil and the Riva ☎ No phone

Matuško Vina

At the heart of the Pelješac Peninsula, the village of Potomje is the centre of wine production and this small winery sells Dingač and Plavac Mali red wines at reasonable prices, plus *prošek* (a sweet aperitif or dessert wine) and liqueurs. The nearby Dingač winery is better known but also more expensive.

✉ Potomje, Pelješac ☎ 020 742393

ENTERTAINMENT

BARS AND NIGHTLIFE

Carpe Diem

Groovy seafront cocktail bar where the beautiful people meet in summer for jazz and Latin nights, full moon and trendy "après-beach" parties.

✉ Riva, Hvar Town ☎ 021 742369; www.carpe-diem-hvar.com 🕐 Summer daily 9am–3am

The Garden

Part-owned by British reggae musician James Brown, The Garden has quickly become the coolest bar in town. Chill out on a beautiful garden terrace high above the city walls while listening to live music and visiting DJs in summer.

✉ Liburnska Obala 6, Zadar ☎ 023 254509; www.watchthegardengrow.eu/the-garden-zadar 🕐 Summer daily 10am–1am

CLASSICAL MUSIC AND PERFORMING ARTS

Hvarsko Kazalište

One of the oldest community theatres in Europe, opened in 1612 and beautifully restored. Performances are staged throughout the summer season.

✉ Trg Svetog Stjepana, Hvar ☎ 021 741059

Hrvatsko Narodno Kazalište Split

The Dalmatian branch of the Croatian National Theatre brings a regular roster of theatre, opera and ballet to Split. This is very much the hub of Split's cultural life.

✉ Trg Gaje Bulata 1, Split ☎ 021 344999; www.hnk-split.hr

Zagreb and Inland Croatia

The vast inland region known as continental Croatia has a very different feel to the fashionable Adriatic coast. Life is harsh here – tourism has made little impact and the effects of the recent war are still visible, particularly along the historic Military Frontier that forms the border with Bosnia and Serbia.

This is a region of contrasting landscapes, from the rolling hills of Zagorje to the fertile farmland of Slavonia and the flood plains of the Danube, Drava and Sava rivers, as well as Croatia's most remarkable natural sight, the waterfalls at the Plitvice Lakes National Park. At the heart of it all is Zagreb, the lively modern capital, whose splendid Habsburg-era architecture is an illustration of the historic links between Croatia and central Europe.

After living for centuries in the shadow of Vienna, Budapest and Belgrade, Zagreb is finally coming into its own. As home to one in four of Croatia's population, the city has a thriving cultural scene and a vibrant cafe life on its streets and squares. Don't ignore the other former Austro-Hungarian cities of inland Croatia – handsome Varaždin with its magnificent baroque architecture, and Osijek, the Slavonian capital, now recovering after the war.

ZAGREB

Zagreb can be neatly divided into two, Gornji Grad (Upper Town) and Donji Grad (Lower Town). Gornji Grad is the site of the original city, founded as a hilltop fortress in the 11th century and still an enchanting district of medieval houses and cobbled streets. Modern Zagreb is centred around Donji Grad, laid out during the 19th century. Between the two is Trg Bana Jelačića, Zagreb's central square.

www.zagreb-touristinfo.hr

6C

Trg Bana Jelačića 11; tel: 01 481 4051

Arheološki Muzej (Archaeological Museum)

This well laid-out museum, with captions in Croatian and English, contains archaeological finds from prehistoric to Roman times. The displays start on the third floor, where you will find the star attraction, the Vučedol dove. This ceramic pot in the shape of a bird, decorated with grooved geometric designs, was excavated near Vukovar and dates back more than 4,000 years. A nearby cabinet contains the complete grave goods of a married couple from the same time, including incense burners, bowls and cups. From the Bronze Age come hoards of gold jewellery and the Idol of Dalj, a carved and engraved female figure from the 14th century BC. The museum also contains the Zagreb Mummy, brought back from Egypt in 1848 and later discovered to be wrapped in a linen shroud on which is inscribed the world's longest surviving example of Etruscan text.

www.amz.hr

Zagreb 4d Trg Nikole Šubića Zrinskog 19 01 487 3101 Tue–Wed and Fri 10–5, Thu 10–8, Sat–Sun 10–1 Moderate Lapidarium courtyard cafe (€) Tram 6, 13

Atelijer Meštrović (Meštrović Studio)

The former home and studio of the Croatian sculptor Ivan Meštrović (1883–1962) now contains an excellent museum of his work, with more than 100 sculptures in wood, bronze and stone displayed in the courtyard, garden and house alongside the artist's original furniture. Common subjects include religious imagery and female nudes, as well as some intimate studies of his own family.

www.mdc.hr/mestrovic/

Zagreb 3e Ulica Mletačka 8 01 485 1123 Tue–Fri 10–6, Sat–Sun 10–2 Moderate

Botanički Vrt (Botanical Garden)
With waterlily-covered lakes, an arboretum and glasshouses containing native plants, this landscaped garden, laid out in 1889, provides an oasis of calm a short distance from the busy roads and railway lines of Donji Grad. It forms the centrepiece of the "Green Horseshoe", a U-shaped promenade of parks and squares designed to ease the pressure on the growing city.
www.botanic.hr
Zagreb 3b Trg Marka Marulića 01 489 8060 Apr–Oct Mon–Tue 9–2:30, Wed–Sun 9–7 Free Tram 2, 4, 9

Etnografski Muzej (Ethnographic Museum)
The parks of Donji Grad are surrounded by grand Austro-Hungarian buildings in the Vienna Secession, or art nouveau styles, many of them built after the earthquake of 1880 to house the city's great museums and cultural institutions. This one, designed as a congress hall, now features displays of folk costume, jewellery and musical instruments from the various regions of Croatia. Across the square is the Hrvatsko Narodno Kazalište (Croatian National Theatre), a typically ostentatious opera house dating from 1895.
www.mdc.hr/etno/
Zagreb 2c Mažuranićev trg 14 01 482 6220 Tue–Thu 10–6, Fri–Sun 10–1 Inexpensive (free on Thu) Tram 12, 13, 14, 17

GORNJI GRAD

Best places to see, ➤ 38–39.

Groblje Mirogoj (Mirogoj Cemetery)

Not many cemeteries are listed as tourist attractions, but this peaceful graveyard on the outskirts of Zagreb is undoubtedly a special place. It was designed by Hermann Bollé (1845–1926), who

also worked on the cathedral, as a resting-place for the citizens of Zagreb. Behind a high wall topped by green cupolas, Catholic, Orthodox, Muslim and Jewish tombstones are found side by side, along with others adorned with the five-pointed Communist star. The arcades to either side of the main entrance contain some impressive monuments to members of Croatia's noble families. Among those buried here is Franjo Tuđman (1922–99), the first president of independent Croatia, whose black granite tomb attracts numerous visitors to light candles and lay flowers at his grave.

Zagreb 4f (off map) 2km (1.25 miles) north of centre Daily 8–6 Free Bus 106 from cathedral

Hrvatski Muzej Naivne Umjetnosti (Croatian Naïve Art Museum)

The Croatian naïve art movement originated in the 1930s in Hlebine (➤ 138) and soon developed an international reputation. The self-taught peasant artists used simple techniques to portray scenes of rural life. This small museum contains a good overview of the movement, including its two key figures Ivan Generalić (1914–92) and his son Josip Generalić (1936–2004).

www.hmnu.org

Zagreb 3e Ulica Sv Ćirila i Metoda 3 01 485 1911 Tue–Fri 10–6, Sat–Sun 10–1 Moderate

Katedrala (Cathedral)

The twin spires of Zagreb's cathedral tower over the city, dominating the views as you approach. It is dedicated to St Stephen and St Ladislaus. There was a church here as early as 1102, but the present neo-Gothic cathedral was built 800 years later by the architect Hermann Bollé following an earthquake which destroyed much of Zagreb in 1880. Behind the altar is the sarcophagus of Cardinal Alojzije Stepinac (1898–1960), a former archbishop of Zagreb who was placed under house arrest by the Tito régime; he was beatified by Pope John Paul II during a visit to Croatia in 1988, the first step on the road to sainthood. His actual tomb, in the north wall, features a relief by Ivan Meštrović, depicting the bishop kneeling humbly before Christ. The nearby sacristy contains some 13th-century frescoes from an earlier cathedral on this site.

Zagreb 5e Kaptol 31 01 481 4727 Mon–Sat 10–5, Sun 1–5 Free Tram 1, 6, 11, 12, 13, 14, 17 to Trg Bana Jelačića

Kula Lotrščak (Burglars' Tower)

The firing of the Grič cannon from the Burglars' Tower at midday has become an essential feature of Zagreb life and it is worth timing your visit to coincide with the ritual. The tower, which takes its name from the "bell of thieves" that once chimed each night as a warning at the closing of the city gates, is the only remaining part of the 13th-century fortifications. It is said that the citizens of Zagreb set their watches when they hear the blast. Climb the spiral staircase just before noon to watch the ceremony, performed by a cannoneer in blue uniform, then continue to the observation platform for the best city views.

Zagreb 3e Strossmayerovo Šetalište 9 01 485 1926 Apr–Oct Tue–Sun 11–7 Inexpensive Funicular to Gradec

Maksimirski Perivoj (Maksimir Park)

When the people of Zagreb want to relax, they hop on a tram to the leafy and relaxed leisure oasis that is Maksimir Park. At weekends the park is crowded out with local families who come here to walk, cycle and enjoy the fresh air. Opened in 1794, this was one of the first public parks in Europe, and with its belvederes, follies, bridges and lakeside paths it retains an enjoyably old-fashioned feel. Children will enjoy the zoo, with its surprisingly large collection of animals including lions, tigers, elephants and bears. Just across from the park is the Maksimir Stadium, home of the Croatian national football team and the local favourites Dinamo Zagreb.

Zagreb 8e (off map) Maksimirska Cesta Tram 11,12

Zoo

01 230 2199 Daily 9–8 in summer, 9–5 in winter (ticket office closed one hour before closing times) Moderate

Medvednica

The mountain range of Medvednica overlooks Zagreb to the north, offering numerous hiking trails and woodland paths within easy reach of the city. It is quite an effort to get there but the journey is all part of the fun. Take tram 8 or 14 to the Mihaljevac terminus, then transfer to tram 15 for the short hop to Dolje. From here, walk through a tunnel and climb a short path to reach the lower station for the *žičara* (cable car). The cars leave on the hour for the 20-minute ascent to the summit of Sljeme (1,035m/ 3,396ft), with dramatic views all the way. There are restaurants near the summit, shady picnic meadows and in winter there are even ski slopes here. A short walk leads to the Church of Our Lady of Sljeme, built in 1932 to celebrate 1,000 years of Christianity in Croatia. If you are feeling energetic, take the cable-car to the summit and walk back down through the beech woods, passing the reconstructed Zrinski silver mine and the 13th-century fortress at Medvedgrad, with panoramic views over the city.

www.pp-medvednica.hr

6B 01 458 6317 Tram 15 then cable car

Muzej Grada Zagreba (Zagreb City Museum)

This enjoyable museum manages the difficult task of bringing Zagreb's complex history to life through an entertaining series of models, reconstructions, themed galleries and interactive displays. Much of the material is arranged chronologically, but there are also rooms devoted to topics such as shopping, theatres, clubs and societies, war and daily life. The tour of the museum, housed in a 17th-century convent, begins with a walk through an Iron Age metal workshop, recently excavated beneath the site. From the founding of Zagreb in 1094 and the "free and royal city" of Gradec in 1242, the museum tells the story of Zagreb up to 1991, when Serbian rockets hit the nearby presidential palace. The event is recalled with video footage and a poignant display of broken crockery and furniture.

www.mgz.hr

Zagreb 4f Ulica Opatička 20 01 485 1364 Tue–Wed and Fri 10–6, Thu 10–10, Sat–Sun 10–1 Moderate Stara Vura restaurant (€€) and cafe (€)

Muzej Mimara (Mimara Museum)

This extensive museum is based on the personal collection of the Croatian businessman Ante Topić

Mimara (1898–1987), who spent his life amassing an eclectic range of artworks from around the world. He donated them to the nation before his death. The extraordinary collection includes ancient Egyptian glassware, Chinese and Japanese porcelain, Persian carpets, Russian and Byzantine icons, a carved ivory English hunting-horn, Italian Renaissance painting and sculpture, and works by Rubens, Rembrandt and Renoir.

Zagreb 2c Rooseveltov Trg 4 01 482 8100
Tue–Wed and Fri–Sat 10–5, Thu 10–7, Sun 10–2
Moderate Cafe (€)
Tram 12, 13, 14, 17

Strossmayerova Galerija Starih Majstora (Strossmayer Gallery of Old Masters)

Bellini, Botticelli, Carpaccio, Lippi, Tintoretto – the great painters of the Italian Renaissance also worked in Croatia and this gallery clearly indicates Croatia's role in the mainstream of European art. It was founded in 1868 by Bishop Josip Juraj Strossmayer (1815–1905), a leading Croatian nationalist and supporter of Croat-Serb unity. A statue of Strossmayer by Ivan Meštrović stands outside the building. Look in the entrance lobby for the Baška stone, an 11th-century tablet from the island of Krk containing the oldest known example of the Glagolitic script. South of here, beyond the ornate cream-coloured Art Pavilion, is an equestrian statue of Tomislav, the first king of Croatia, crowned in AD925.

www.mdc.hr/strossmayer

Zagreb 4c Trg Nikole Šubića Zrinskog 11 01 481 3344 Tue 10–1, 5–7, Wed–Sun 10–1 Inexpensive Tram 6, 13

Trg Bana Jelačića

With its modern trams, newspaper kiosks, flower stalls and open-air cafés, this broad square is the focal point of Zagreb and the best place to take the pulse of the city. This is where people meet to start the evening *korzo*, a ritual stroll to see and be seen. At the centre of the square is an equestrian statue of Governor Josip Jelačić (1801–59), an iconic figure in Croatian nationalism; during the Tito years, the statue was removed and dismantled but it was returned here in 1990. Just above the square, on a raised terrace, is Zagreb's colourful central market, where farmers sell fresh produce on weekday mornings.

Zagreb 4d Tram 1, 6, 11, 12, 13, 14, 17

Trg Bana Jelačića 11; tel: 01 481 4051

a walk around Zagreb Old Town

This short walk takes you from Trg Bana Jelačića into the heart of Gornji Grad, with the option of a funicular ride. The best time for walking is during the early evening, joining the citizens of Zagreb on their *korzo* or promenade.

Start in Trg Bana Jelačića and head west along Ilica, Zagreb's main shopping street. Take the first right into Ulica Tomića, usually known as Tomićeva.

You can ascend to the Upper Town by funicular or by climbing the flight of steps. Either way, you arrive on the Strossmayerovo Šetalište promenade, opposite Kula Lotrščak (➤ 127).

Continue straight ahead beside the tower, passing a Greek Orthodox church and the Croatian Naïve Art Museum (➤ 125) to arrive in Markov trg (St Mark's Square), dominated by the colourful roof tiles of St Mark's Church.

This square is the heart of the Croatian government, with the presidential palace on your left and the Sabor (Parliament) on your right.

Turn right along Ulica Kamenita and walk through the Kamenita Vrata (Stone Gate), where pilgrims light candles at the shrine. Take the steps to the right beside a statue of George and the Dragon to walk down Ulica Radićva. Turn left onto Krvavi Most (Bloody Bridge) and cross the bridge to reach Ulica Tkalčiceva, a pretty street of 19th-century houses and trendy open-air bars. Continue straight ahead to reach the upper level of Dolac market, then take the steps down to your right to return to Trg Bana Jelačića.

Distance 2km (1.25 miles)
Time 1 hour
Start/end point Trg Bana Jelačića *Zagreb 4d*
Tram 1, 6, 11, 13, 14, 17
Lunch Kerempuh (€€); Dolac market; tel: 01 481 9000

Inland Croatia

ČAKOVEC

Čakovec is the main town of the Međimurje, a region of fertile farmland between the Mura and Drava rivers close to the Hungarian border. The town's history dates to 1546, when the Hapsburg emperor Ferdinand I awarded it to the Zrinski family in recognition of their services in battles against the Ottoman Turks. Their **castle** is now the Museum of the Međimurje, with an enjoyable collection of Carnival masks, a recreated pharmacy and works by local artists. Zrinski Park, between the castle and town centre, contains a monument to Nikola Zrinski (1620–64), a governor of Croatia who was killed by a wild boar while out hunting.

6A Bus from Varaždin

Trg Kralja Tomislava 1; tel: 040 313319

Castle

Tue–Fri 10–3, Sat–Sun 10–1

Inexpensive

ĐAKOVO

If you are driving around eastern Slavonia, Đakovo makes a good place to spend the night or to break the journey back to Zagreb. The main sight is the red-brick cathedral, whose twin spires, 84m (275ft) tall, tower over the city. This is the third cathedral on the site; it was built between 1866 and 1882 by Bishop Josip Juraj Strossmayer, a leading figure in 19th-century Croatian nationalism. A short walk along Ulica Matije Gupca leads to a Lippizaner stud farm, where the famous white horses are bred and trained.

www.tz-djakovo.hr

10C

Ulica Kralja Tomislava 3; tel: 031 812319

HLEBINE

The village of Hlebine was the birthplace of naïve art in Croatia and it is still home to several painters and sculptors producing vivid scenes of rural life. Their work can be seen at **Galerija Hlebine,** which also has a room devoted to Ivan Generalić (1914–92), considered the father of the Croatian naïve art movement.

7B

Galerija Hlebine

Trg Ivana Generalića 15 048 836075 Mon–Fri 10–4, Sat 10–2 Inexpensive

KOPAČKI RIT, PARK PRIRODE

Situated on the border with Serbia at the confluence of the Danube and Drava rivers, the Kopački Rit wetlands (or nature park, *park prirode*), which forms a valuable wildlife habitat for numerous species of nesting and migrant birds, is becoming increasingly popular with both mainstream tourists and dedicated ornithologists. Get there by following signs from Bilje, 8km (5 miles) north of Osijek on the main road to Hungary. On a brief visit, start with a boat trip on the *Orao I*, which leaves from a jetty near the park entrance. Herons and cormorants are common, and you may see kingfishers and black storks. Deeper into the park are footpaths which lead through poplar and oak forests, where the Hapsburg aristocracy used to hunt deer and wild boar. The visitor centre at the park entrance is a good source of information, maps and souvenirs.

www.kopacki-rit.com

11B 031 752320 Daily 9–5 Cafe (€) at park entrance; Kormoran restaurant (€€) inside the park Boat trips Apr–Oct three or four times daily Expensive

KRAPINA

The town at the centre of the Zagorje region (➤ 149) is famous for the discovery of *Homo Krapinensis* (Krapina Man), a Neanderthal human who lived in caves some 30,000 years ago and whose remains were excavated and studied by Croatian archaeologist Dragutin Gorjanović Kramberger in 1899. Around 900 human bones were unearthed on the Hušnjakovo hill, making it one of the richest collections of human fossils in the world, though unfortunately a complete skeleton was never found. Most of the originals are now kept in the Croatian Natural History Museum in Zagreb, though the **Muzej Evolucije** (Museum of Evolution) in Krapina has reproductions of skulls and bones from various mammals, including wolves, bears, rhino and deer. A path behind the museum leads up the hill to the cave where the bones were discovered, now marked by somewhat artificial sculptures of prehistoric cavemen and animals.

5B Bus from Zagreb Train from Zagreb

Muzej Evolucije

Šetalište V Sluge 049 371491 Apr–Sep daily 9–5; Oct–Mar Tue–Sun 10–3 Moderate

KUMROVEC

This small village close to the Slovenian border is best known as the birthplace of Josip Broz Tito. Tito may have brought all the disparate elements of Yugoslavia together, but this fascinating site illuminates his traditional Croatian upbringing. These days, people come here for two reasons – to pay homage to the former Yugoslav leader and to experience the feel of rural life at the turn of the 20th century, when Tito was growing up here. The house in which he was born stands near the entrance to the village, with a statue

outside and an exhibition inside giving a slightly revisionist account of Tito's place in history.

A short walk along the main street leads to the school, which Tito attended from 1900 to 1905. However, the main interest is in wandering around the **Staro Selo** (Old Village), where cottages, farmhouses, granaries, barns and stables have been restored as an open-air museum of rural life. Among them is the blacksmith's workshop once owned by Tito's family. In summer, there are exhibitions of craftmaking (pottery, weaving, wooden toys, wine, cider) in the various studios and an old wine-cellar serving cottage cheese parcels from Zagorje. Despite the theme-park atmosphere, Kumrovec is still a working agricultural village and you see farmers on tractors and in the fields side by side with the museum exhibits.

5B Bus from Zagreb

Staro Selo

049 225830; www.mdc.hr/kumrovec Apr–Sep daily 9–7; Oct–Mar 9–4

Moderate

LONJSKO POLJE, PARK PRIRODE

The flood plains of the River Sava have been designated a nature park *(park prirode)*, preserving not only a fragile environment but also a peaceful way of life. Visitors come here in spring and summer to see the nesting white storks, one of the largest populations in Europe. Between April and August, almost every house in the village of Čigoć has a stork's nest on the roof. The people of the Lonjsko Polje live in traditional oak cottages, with external wooden staircases leading up to the first floor and chimney-less attics where hams and sausages are cured. There are good examples in all villages, but most are in Čigoć and Krapje. Just outside Krapje is Krapje Đol, Croatia's first ornithological reserve, where herons and other waterfowl can often be seen. The **information centre** in Čigoć has maps of local walks.

www.pp-lonjsko-polje.hr

7C Moderate

Information centre

Čigoć 26 044 715115 Daily 8–4

MARIJA BISTRICA

Croatia's leading Marian shrine is situated north of Zagreb at the entrance to the Zagorje (► 149). Catholic pilgrims from Croatia and abroad come here to pay homage to a dark wooden statue of the Virgin to which miraculous powers have been attributed. The present church was built to house the statue in 1883 and was designed by Hermann Bollé, architect of Zagreb cathedral. On feast days, huge open-air masses are held in the amphitheatre behind the church. You can climb the Via Crucis (Way of the Cross) for the best views. Shops in the main square sell religious souvenirs as well as giant decorated gingerbread hearts, a speciality of this region.

6B Bus from Zagreb

Zagrebačka 66; tel: 049 468380

NACIONALNI PARK PLITVIČKA JEZERA

Best places to see, ➤ 46–47.

OSIJEK

The largest city in eastern Croatia stands on the south bank of the River Drava. The main attraction is Tvrđa, an 18th-century fortress town 2km (1.25 miles) east of the centre. Heavily damaged by shelling in 1991, this is now an enjoyable district of cobbled streets, churches, palaces and defensive walls. At the centre of the main square is a plague column, erected in 1729 to give thanks for deliverance from the disease. A

riverside footpath connects Tvrđa to the city centre; you can cross the suspension bridge to reach the north bank for views across the river. Osijek makes a good base for visiting the Kopački Rit Nature Park (➤ 138).

11C

Županijska 2; tel: 031 203755; www.tzosbarzup.hr

SAMOBOR

This pleasing country town is just 20km (12.5 miles) from Zagreb, making it a popular day out from the capital. Pretty, pastel-coloured town houses surround the main square, where a stream runs beneath an onion-domed church. Viennese-style pastry shops around the square sell *samoborska kremšnita*, a rich custard and cream tart. The town has an air of prosperity, helped by weekend visitors from Slovenia, Austria and Zagreb. Just outside Samobor are the green hills of the Žumberak-Samoborsko Gorje Nature Park.

5C Bus from Zagreb

Trg Kralja Tomislava 5; tel: 01 336 0044

SLAVONSKI BROD

This intriguing town on the River Sava grew up around its star-shaped fortress, built in the 18th century on the Military Frontier between the Ottoman and Hapsburg empires. During the recent war, the fortress was repeatedly attacked from across the river by Bosnian Serbs in the town of Bosanski Brod. Slavonski Brod is currently undergoing extensive reconstruction. A short walk along the riverbank leads to an 18th-century Franciscan monastery with a peaceful cloister at its centre.

10D Bus from Zagreb

Trg Pobjede 30; tel: 035 445765; www.tzgsb.hr

TRAKOŠĆAN

One of the best-known sights in Croatia is this fairy-tale castle, standing proud on a wooded hillside, its white walls, battlements and towers reflected in an artificial lake. Although the castle dates from the 13th century, its current appearance is the result of 19th-century restoration by the owners, the Drašković family. Confiscated by the state during the Tito years, the castle is now a museum of aristocratic life, its salons filled with family portraits, firearms and antique furniture. There are walks in the parkland, and a path leads around the lake; in summer there is also a floating café with pedal-boats to rent.

www.trakoscan.hr

5B 042 796422 Apr–Sep daily 9–6; Oct–Mar 9–3 Moderate

VARAŽDIN

Best places to see, ➤ 52–53.

VELIKI TABOR

This fine 16th-century castle stands on a hill above the village of Desinić. The displays are not as interesting as those at Trakošćan (➤ 146) and the castle is not as well preserved, but it is worth visiting for the magnificent views across the Zagorje (➤ 149) from the semicircular towers. Occasional displays of swordsmanship are held in the courtyard by actors in military costume.

www.velikitabor.com

5B 049 343963 Apr–Sep daily 10–5; Oct–Mar 9–3 Inexpensive

VUKOVAR

A visit to Vukovar is a powerful, moving experience and a chance to understand why this small town on the Danube plays such an important part in the Croatian psyche. For three months in 1991, it came under siege from Serbian forces; deprived of food and

water, the inhabitants were forced out of their homes. Many escaped to safety across the cornfields but at least 2,000 people were killed and their bodies dumped in mass graves. Few of the survivors have returned and many of the houses are no more than empty shells. A bleak memorial by the riverbank pays tribute to the dead. In the town cemetery, on the road to Ilok, rows of unmarked white crosses record the victims who were never found. Vukovar today is trying to become the grand baroque town it once was and tourism has an essential part to play in this renaissance.

www.turizamvukovar.hr

12C

Strossmayerova 15; tel: 032 442889

ZAGORJE

With its rolling green meadows, hilltop castles and churches, vineyards, pretty villages and spa towns, the Zagorje region, north of Zagreb, is a place of legendary beauty in Croatia. The main attractions are the castles at Trakošćan (➤ 146) and Veliki Tabor (➤ opposite), the pilgrimage church at Marija Bistrica (➤ 143) and the ethnographic museum at Kumrovec (➤ 140), but the real appeal of this region lies in getting off the beaten track and soaking up the atmosphere of bucolic rural life.

5B

HOTELS

KOPAČKI RIT

Galić (€)

Simple rooms in a bungalow attached to a family home in the village of Bilje, 4km (2.5 miles) from the entrance to the nature park. Includes home-made breakfast.

✉ Ritska 1, Bilje ☎ 031 750393

LONJSKO POLJE

Ravlić (€)

Cosy farmhouse accommodation on the top floor of a wooden cottage with views over the river. Excellent home-cooking but the bathroom is outdoors.

✉ Mužilovčica 72 ☎ 044 710151

OSIJEK

Hotel Osijek (€€€)

This modern four-star tower hotel has all mod cons and a good location in the centre of Osijek. Modest wellness centre.

✚ Šamačka 4 ☎ 031 230 333; www.hotelosijek.hr

Waldinger (€€)

Capture the feel of 19th-century Osijek by staying at this charming small hotel in an art nouveau building with a Viennese-style cafe.

✉ Županijska 8 ☎ 031 250450; www.waldinger.hr

PLITVIČKA JEZERA

Jezero (€€)

The biggest and best of the three hotels inside the national park, with views, sauna and steam baths.

✉ Plitvička Jezera ☎ 053 751400; www.np-plitvicka-jezera.hr

SAMOBOR

Livadić (€)

Charming, family-run hotel on the main square, with a Viennese-style salon and courtyard serving delicious coffee and cakes.

✉ Trg Kralja Tomislava 1 ☎ 01 336 5850; www.hotel-livadic.hr

VARAŽDIN

Maltar (€)

Modest hotel with simply furnished rooms, a short walk from the town centre. This family-run hotel also offers breakfast, lunch and dinner, with some suites available for those looking to enjoy a little more space.

✉ Ulica Prešernova 1 ☎ 042 311100; www.maltar.hr

Hotel Turist (€€)

This modern and perfectly comfortable hotel has 104 rooms set in a handy location in Varaždin. The old town is a short stroll away, while there is parking and easy access to the roads out of town, making this a good base for exploring the Zagorje.

✚ Aleja Kralja Zvonimira 1 ☎ 042 395 395; www.hotel-turist.hr

VUKOVAR

Lav (€€)

Completely destroyed during the war, this hotel was rebuilt and reopened in 2005 as a symbol of Vukovar's resilience. Some of the comfortable rooms look out over the River Danube.

✉ Strossmayerova 18 ☎ 032 445100; www.hotel-lav.hr

ZAGORJE

Dvorac Bežanec (€€)

Croatia's top country-house hotel is set in a mansion near Pregrada, with antique furniture, fine food and wine. The rooms are woven around a castle, which dates back as far as the 17th century, making this a thoroughly unique place to stay. Sports facilities include tennis, horse-riding and archery.

✉ Valentinovo 55, Pregrada ☎ 049 376800; www.bezanec.hr

ZAGREB

Arcotel Allegra (€€€)

Billed as Zagreb's first design hotel, this offers 151 rooms with contemporary furnishings, DVD player and internet connection. Close to the bus and railway stations.

✉ Branimirova 29 ☎ 01 469 6000; www.arcotel.at/allegra

Central (€€)

The location next to the railway station in the centre of town helps attract tourists and budget-conscious business people to this simple, but efficient hotel. All rooms have satellite TV and internet connections, while some guests might be tempted by the rather unusual array of gambling machines on the site too.

Branimirova 3 01 484 1122; www.hotel-central.hr

Dubrovnik (€€€)

Built in 1929 and recently restored, this is the most centrally located of the top-of-the-range hotels. Some of the rooms overlook the main square.

Ulica Ljudevita Gaja 1 01 486 3555; www.hotel-dubrovnik.hr

Ilica (€€)

This small, friendly hotel has just 12 rooms, and is on Zagreb's main shopping street a short walk from Trg Bana Jelačića. A good budget choice in the heart of the city.

Ilica 102 01 377 7522; www.hotel-ilica.hr

Jägerhorn (€€)

Small, simply furnished hotel set around a courtyard just off the main square. The hotel claims to be the city's oldest, dating back as far as 1827. The restaurant here is famed for its game dishes.

Ilica 14 01 483 3877; www.hotel-pansion-jaegerhorn.hr

Movie Hotel (€€)

This theme hotel is located above a popular English-style pub. Rooms are named after film stars and decorated with movie posters.

Savska Cesta 141 01 600 3600; www.themoviehotel.com

Palace (€€€)

The oldest hotel in Zagreb opened in 1907 and it is still full of old-world charm, with antique furniture, Viennese salons and views over a peaceful green park.

Strossmayerova Trg 10 01 489 96001; www.palace.hr

Regent Esplanade (€€€)
Traditionally the top address in town, this luxury hotel near the railway station is the meeting-place of the rich and famous of Zagreb. Spacious and lavishly furnished rooms and suites are complemented by a health club and a choice of bars.
✉ Mihanovićeva 1 ☎ 01 456 6666; www.theregentzagreb.com

Sliško (€€)
Small, family-run hotel with simple but comfortable rooms in a quiet street close to the bus station, a 20-minute walk or a short tram ride from the centre.
✉ Ulica Supilova 13 ☎ 01 618 4777; www.slisko.hr

Westin Zagreb (€€€)
This high-rise hotel is firmly aimed at business travellers, with facilities including solarium, fitness centre and internet access.
✉ Kršnjavoga 1 ☎ 01 489 2000; www.westin.com/zagreb

RESTAURANTS

KOPAČKI RIT

Kod Varge (€)
Fiery *kulen* (salami), *fiš paprikaš* (fish casserole) and fried carp from local rivers are the specialities at this family-run tavern in the village of Bilje.
✉ Ulica Kralja Zvonimira 37A, Bilje ☎ 031 750120 🕓 Daily 8am–11pm

OSIJEK

Alas (€€)
A must for fish lovers. The key dish here is a spicy paprika-laden casserole where the main attraction is local catfish – they lay on bibs as things can get a little messy. It comes, as many dishes do, with tasty home-made noodles. Some decent wines and modest prices make this a winner.
✚ Reisnerova 12a, Osijek ☎ 031 21 30 32

Slavonska Kuča (€€)
Cosy little place on the edge of the Tvrđa fortress, serving typically

spicy Slavonian country cooking such as *čobanec*, a meat stew flavoured with paprika.

✉ Ulica Firingera 26 ☎ 031 369955 ⌚ Mon–Sat 9am–11pm

SAMOBOR

Kavana Livadić (€)

The best of the Viennese-style pastry shops around Samobor's main square, offering tempting treats such as *samoborska kremšnita* (custard tart).

✉ Trg Kralja Tomislava 1 ☎ 01 336 5850 ⌚ Daily 8am–11pm

Pri Staroj Vuri (€€)

Smart, traditional restaurant in a mustard-coloured town house behind the church, specializing in grilled meat and fish dishes from the days of the Habsburg empire.

✉ Ulica Giznik 2 ☎ 01 336 0548; www.pri-staroj-vuri.hr ⌚ Mon–Sat 11–11, Sun 11–6

Samoborska Pivnica (€)

Cavernous beer hall set just back from the main square, with an emphasis on simple meat dishes such as beef tongue and local sausages served with strong Samobor mustard.

✉ Šmidhenova 3 ☎ 01 336 1623; www.samoborska-pivnica.hr ⌚ Daily 9am–11pm

VARAŽDIN

Zlatna Guška (€€€)

Relive the days of the Austro-Hungarian empire in this atmospheric cellar restaurant, with pikestaffs on the walls and ancient recipes such as beef daggers and nettle soup.

✉ Habdelićeva 4 ☎ 042 213393 ⌚ Daily 10am–11pm

ZAGORJE

Grešna Gorica (€)

Farmhouse restaurant offering rustic casseroles and game dishes such as venison goulash, on a terrace with views to Veliki Tabor.

✉ Taborgradska 3, Desinić ☎ 049 343001 ⌚ Daily 10–10

ZAGREB

Baltazar (€€)

Traditional restaurant specializing in grilled meat in a courtyard near the cathedral.

✉ Nova Ves 4 ☎ 01 466 6999; www.restoran-baltazar.hr 🕒 Mon–Sat 12–12

Boban (€€)

Trendy Italian cellar restaurant and bar in a pedestrian street just off Trg Bana Jelačića. Well-deserved reputation for pasta and grills.

✉ Ulica Ljudevita Gaja 9 ☎ 01 481 1549; www.boban.hr 🕒 Daily 11am–midnight

Ivica i Marica (€€)

Organic and vegetarian dishes, plus a handful of meat and fish choices, at this fairy-tale cottage restaurant and cake shop on Zagreb's busy nightlife strip.

✉ Tkalčićeva 70 ☎ 01 482 8999; www.ivicaimarica.com 🕒 Daily noon–11pm

K Pivovari (€€)

Rustic food and a great choice of beers at a pub attached to Zagreb's oldest brewery. Savour steaks, sausages and baked potatoes washed down with Ožujsko or Tomislav beer.

✉ Ilica 222 ☎ 01 375 1808; www.kpivovari.com 🕒 Mon–Sat 10am–midnight, Sun 10–5

Kerempuh (€€)

Busy restaurant on the upper level of Dolac market, offering fresh produce from the market stalls below. Get here early for a seat on the terrace. Lunch only

✉ Dolac market ☎ 01 481 9000 🕒 Mon–Sat 9–4

Paviljon (€€€)

Refined menu of Italian and Central European cuisine in the ornate Art Pavilion, built in 1896 in a park opposite the railway station.

✉ Trg Kralja Tomislava 22 ☎ 01 481 3066 🕒 Mon–Sat 12–12

Pod Gričkim Topom (€€)
Romantic restaurant serving grilled meat, fish and traditional cuisine on a terrace overlooking the city from Gornji Grad.
✉ Zakmardijeve Stube 5 (beside upper funicular terminus) ☎ 01 483 3607
🕐 Mon–Sat 11am–midnight, Sun 11–5

Rubelj (€)
One of several down-to-earth grills on a terrace beneath Dolac market, offering a simple but delicious range of *ćevapčići* and kebabs served in huge crusty rolls.
✉ Dolac 2 ☎ 01 481 8777; www.rubelj-grill.hr 🕐 Daily 8am–11pm

Vallis Aurea (€)
Spicy Slavonian home cooking at decent prices, in a cosy tavern with wooden tables near the foot of the funicular to Gornji Grad.
✉ Ulica Tomića 4 ☎ 01 483 1305 🕐 Mon–Sat 9am–11pm

Vincek (€)
Delicious cakes and pastries and wonderful ice-creams at this popular *slastičarnica* near Trg Bana Jelačića.
✉ Ilica 18 ☎ 01 483 3612; www.vincek.com.hr 🕐 Mon–Sat 9am–11pm

SHOPPING

BOOKS

Algoritam
Large bookshop in the base of the Hotel Dubrovnik, with foreign-language books and magazines in the basement.
✉ Ulica Ljudevita Gaja 1, Zagreb ☎ 01 488 1555

FASHION ACCESSORIES

Croata
Silk ties, scarves and accessories sold in the home of the tie. The main branch is in the Oktogon passage near Trg Bana Jelačića. There are other branches in Dubrovnik, Split, Rijeka, Osijek, Varaždin and at airports.
✉ Prolaz Oktogon, Ilica 5; also at Kaptol 13, Zagreb ☎ 01 481 2726; www.croata.hr

FOOD AND DRINK

Dolac Market

The city's main market is located on a raised terrace above Trg Bana Jelačića. Farmers sell fresh fruit and vegetables at outdoor stalls, with meat, fish, bread and cheese sold from indoor halls.

✉ Dolac, Zagreb 🕒 Mon–Sat 6–2, Sun 7–12

Galerija Pršut

The best range of cured hams from Istria and Dalmatia, plus salami, cheese, wines and olive oil.

✉ Vlaška 7, Zagreb ☎ 01 481 6129

Obitelj Filipec

The Filipec family produce *bermet*, a vermouth flavoured with carob and figs, and *muštarda*, a sweet, spicy grape mustard dating back to a recipe from 1808.

✉ Stražnička 1 (ring the bell), Samobor ☎ 01 336 4835

Vinoteka Bornstein

Large wine cellar near the cathedral selling an extensive range of Croatian wines, spirits and liqueurs. Look out the crisp, dry wines of the coast, that work well with seafood, the mighty reds of Dalmatia and the sweet dessert wines of Slavonia.

✉ Kaptol 19, Zagreb ☎ 01 481 2361; www.bornstein.hr

ENTERTAINMENT

BARS AND NIGHTLIFE

ZAGREB

The liveliest streets are Tkalčićeva in the upper town, and Bogovićeva, just off Trg Bana Jelačića. Tkalčićeva is more youthful, fashionable and edgy, while Bogovićeva and the surrounding streets and squares are lined with busy open-air cafes and ice-cream parlours attracting a wide range of ages and nationalities.

Aquarius

The top venue for serious clubbers began as a wooden shack on the shores of Lake Jarun, 4km (2.5 miles) south of the city centre.

Today it is a Croatian superclub with a massive following.
✉ Aleja Matije Ljubeka, Lake Jarun ☎ 01 364 0231; www.aquarius.hr
🕐 Tue–Sun 9pm–4am

BP Club

Popular basement jazz club near Trg Bana Jelačića. A mecca for lovers of jazz and anyone looking for a fun night out that comes complete with world-class jazz.
✉ Ulica Nikole Tesle 7, Zagreb ☎ 01 481 4444; www.bpclub.hr 🕐 Daily 5pm–1am

Sax

Live music most nights at this fun venue. Rock and indie with an array of (mainly) Croatian bands/singers; plenty of jazz and blues.
✉ Palmotićeva 22, Zagreb ☎ 01 487 2836; www.sax-zg.hr 🕐 Daily 9am–4am

CLASSICAL MUSIC AND PERFORMING ARTS

Hrvatsko Narodno Kazalište (Croatian National Theatre)

This magnificent 19th-century opera house is the home of serious drama in Zagreb, and also hosts opera and ballet seasons.
✉ Trg Maršala Tita 15, Zagreb ☎ 01 488 8415; www.hnk.hr

Hrvatsko Narodno Kazalište

Restored Hapsburg-era theatre in Osijek. Most performances are in Croatian, but the quality and enthusiasm of the performers usually manages to transcend the language barrier.
✉ Županijska 9, Osijek ☎ 031 220700; www.hnk-osijek.hr

Hrvatsko Narodno Kazalište

Opened in 1873 and still staging classical drama, opera and music. An active player in Varaždin's eclectic range of arts festivals.
✉ Ulica Augusta Cesarca 1, Varaždin ☎ 042 214688; www.hnkvz.hr

Koncertna Dvorana Vatroslav Lisinski

Zagreb's main concert hall is home to the Zagreb Philharmonic Orchestra.
✉ Trg Stjepana Radića 4, Zagreb ☎ 01 612 1167; www.lisinski.hr

Istria and Kvarner

Although it includes some of Croatia's biggest holiday resorts, Istria feels like a different country altogether. Between the world wars, this northern Adriatic peninsula was part of Italy and it is still the most Italian place in Croatia.

Many of the towns have both Italian and Croatian names and the cultural influences owe as much to Venice as to Zagreb. The hill towns of inland Istria, surrounded by vineyards and olive groves, are reminiscent of northern Italy. In summer, the west coast is buzzing with tourists, who fill the waterfront cafes, admire the work of pavement artists and soak up the Mediterranean atmosphere.

Between Istria and Dalmatia is Kvarner bay. Although less well known than the coastal regions to the north and south, Kvarner contains Croatia's two largest islands, Cres and Krk, as well as Rab with its charming medieval capital. Other highlights are the lively port city of Rijeka, the highlands of Gorski Kotar and Risnjak National Park, as well as Croatia's grandest Habsburg-era resort at Opatija.

BUZET

The largest of Istria's hill towns occupies a commanding position high above the River Mirna. The old town is a maze of cobbled streets and squares enclosed by medieval walls and gates. Truffle-hunting is big business around Buzet in autumn. Each September, a giant truffle omelette made with more than 2,000 eggs is cooked on the main square during the annual festival (➤ 25).

www.tz-buzet.hr

2D Bus from Pula, Poreč and Rovinj

Trg Fontana 7; tel: 052 662343

GROŽNJAN (GRISIGNANA)

This charming hilltop village was deserted in the 1960s but has since been discovered by painters and musicians and is now a thriving artists' colony. Each year it becomes the venue for an international summer school of young musicians, and concerts are held in the church on summer evenings. There are few specific sights but this is a lovely place to stroll, checking out the art galleries, sitting beneath the Venetian loggia and watching the sun set from the church terrace with distant views of the sea.

2D

Umberta Gorjana 3; tel: 052 776 131

HUM

Hum's rather dubious claim to fame is that it is "the smallest town in the world", with just 20 inhabitants but annual elections for mayor. In truth, it is just another village of stone houses but a very pretty one at that, with an excellent restaurant which justifies the visit. The road from Roč to Hum is known as Glagolitic Alley, and is lined with sculptures commemorating the Glagolitic script, a 41-letter Slavonic alphabet which was devised by Greek missionaries in the ninth century and used in religious texts in Croatia for a thousand years.

2D

KRK

Croatia's largest island is reached by a toll bridge south of Rijeka. The big draw here is Baška, at the island's southern tip, where one of Croatia's finest sandy beaches faces the Velebit mountains across the water. The capital, Krk town, was an old Roman city and you can still make out sections of the Roman walls. The neighbouring island of Cres has colonies of bottlenose dolphins.

www.tz-krk.hr

3E Bus from Rijeka Ferry from Cres; also from Rab in summer

Obala Hrvatske Mornarice, Krk Town; tel: 051 220 226

MOTOVUN (MONTONA)

The archetypal Istrian hill town perches high above the Mirna valley, dominating the surrounding countryside and oak woods. You enter through the old town gate, lined with Roman carvings and Venetian stone lions, then climb the cobbled streets to the main square. From here, it takes about 10 minutes to make a complete circuit of the ramparts, with magnificent views all the way. In summer, Motovun is extremely popular with day trippers; there are several restaurants specializing in truffle dishes and shops sell local truffles, wine and *biska* (mistletoe brandy).

✚ 2D

ℹ Trg Jozefa Ressela 1; tel: 052 617480

NACIONALNI PARK BRIJUNI

The beautiful island of Veli Brijun was used by the Yugoslav leader Tito as his summer retreat. For six months of every year, he would stay here in his villa, entertaining world leaders and running the country while hunting in his private game reserve. The island is still used by government officials but these days it is also at the centre of a national park. The easiest way to get there is on an official national park **boat trip** from the fishing port of Fažana. This gives you several hours on the island, and the ticket includes a guided tour on a miniature road train. Among the highlights are a golf course, safari park, a Byzantine fortress and a first-century Roman

villa. There is also a museum, with stuffed animals on the ground floor and upstairs photos of Tito with his various visitors, including President Fidel Castro of Cuba and Queen Elizabeth II of Britain, as well as film stars such as Richard Burton, Gina Lollobrigida and Sophia Loren. To explore the island in more depth, you can rent bicycles or electric golf carts, or even take a ride in Tito's 1953 Cadillac.

www.brijuni.hr

2E Cafe (€) at harbour Boat trips from Fažana

Boat trips

Brijunska 10, Fažana 052 525 883 Several times daily in summer, once or twice daily in winter Expensive

OPATIJA

At the turn of the 20th century Opatija was one of Europe's most fashionable resorts, a winter playground for the Austrian royals and Hapsburg aristocracy, who would while away their time in its casinos, gardens and parks. It is still a popular resort, but these days the visitors are more likely to be Croatian honeymooners or week-enders. The grand *fin-de-siècle* villas and hotels still stand on the seafront, reminders of past glory; walk along the Lungomare (➤ 64–65) for a delightful seaside stroll.

www.opatija-tourism.hr

3D Bus from Pula and Rijeka

Maršala Tita 101; tel: 051 271 310

PAZIN (PISINO)

This small town is actually the administrative capital of Istria, chosen because of its central position despite the size and importance of Pula. It is worth a short visit to see the **castle,** which contains the Istria Ethnographic Museum with displays of folk costumes and musical instruments, as well as a room devoted to Juraj Dobrila (1812–82), a local boy who rose to become bishop of Trieste and who is featured on the 10-kuna note.

The castle is situated on a cliff, overlooking a great gorge in the River Pazinčica which is said to have inspired the novelist Jules Verne (1828–1905) – the hero of his novel *Mathias Sandorf* was held prisoner in the castle and escaped by throwing himself into the pit.

2D · Bus from Pula, Poreč and Rovinj

Franine i Jurine 14; tel: 052 622460

Castle

Trg Istarskog Razvoda · Mid-Apr to mid-Oct Tue–Sun 10–6; mid-Oct to mid-Apr Tue–Thu 10–3, Fri 12–5, Sat–Sun 11–5 · Inexpensive

POREČ (PARENZO)

It would be easy to write off Poreč as an ugly example of mass tourism gone too far. This is, after all, Croatia's biggest resort, and the old Roman town is now completely dwarfed by the campsites, hotels and holiday complexes that have grown up around it. In summer, Poreč struggles to cope with an endless tide of visitors, yet at the heart of all this is a well-preserved old town containing one of Croatia's most remarkable attractions – the sixth-century **Basilica of Euphrasius** with its extraordinary mosaics.

The first church on this site was built in the fourth century and dedicated to St Maur, a leader of the underground church who was martyred during the reign of the Roman emperor Diocletian. Some of the mosaics from the original church have survived, and can be seen through gaps in the floor. The real treasures, though, are the Byzantine mosaics in the central apse, richly encrusted with gold leaf. The upper panel depicts Christ with his apostles, while the central section features the Virgin Mary with the baby Jesus in her arms, surrounded by saints and angels including St Maur, and Bishop Euphrasius holding a model of his

basilica. Afterwards, you can climb the bell tower and visit the museum of sacred art in the bishop's palace just off the courtyard.

The old town makes for a pleasant stroll, with a pair of ruined Roman temples and narrow lanes leading off from the original main streets, Cardo and Decumanus. Boats leave from the harbour in summer for the wooded island of Sveti Nikola.

www.to-porec.com

1E Bus from Pula, Rovinj and Vrsar

Zagrebačka 9; tel: 052 451293

Basilica of Euphrasius

Eufrazijeva Daily 8–8 in summer, 10–7 in winter Free (museum and bell tower: inexpensive)

PULA (POLA)

Although the main reason for visiting Pula is to see the Roman arena (➤ 48), there are other Roman sights in town. The first-century Temple of Augustus still on the edge of the old forum, is now a pleasant café-lined square. Not far from here is the Arch of Sergi, erected by a wealthy Roman family in the first century BC in memory of a triumphant battle.

www.pulainfo.hr

2E Bus from Poreč and Rovinj

Forum 3; tel: 052 212 987

PULA ARENA

Best places to see, ➤ 48–49.

RAB

The old Roman city of Arba, now known as Rab, is one of the Adriatic's most charming towns. With four tall Venetian bell towers rising above the rooftops like the masts of a ship, it is at its best when seen from the sea. The old town is set on a narrow peninsula; you can climb part of the medieval walls for the best views.

The island of Rab has some excellent sandy beaches but is perhaps best known as the place where the British king Edward VIII bathed naked in 1936, one of the earliest recorded instances of naturism in Croatia.

www.tzg-rab.hr

4E Bus from Rijeka Ferry from Jablanac; also from Baška on Krk in summer

Trg Municipium Arba 8; tel: 051 724 064

RIJEKA

Croatia's biggest port, Rijeka operates ferries to Split and Dubrovnik. Among the grand Habsburg-era buildings on the waterfront are

the offices of the Jadrolinija ferry company, whose facade features reliefs and sculptures on nautical themes. Just back from the harbour, the Korzo is a busy shopping street and lively promenade. An archway beneath the clock tower leads to the oldest part of the city.

www.tz-rijeka.hr

3D Bus from Pula Train from Zagreb Ferry from Zadar, Split and Dubrovnik

Korzo 33; tel: 051 335882

ROVINJ

Best places to see, ➤ 50–51.

a walk along the Leska Trail

The Risnjak National Park occupies a large area of fir and beech forests in the Gorski Kotar mountain range, just inland from Rijeka. There are numerous challenging walks in the mountains, including a climb to the summit of Veliki Risnjak (1,528m/5,013ft), but this walk is designed to be done by anyone. You will need strong shoes and you should be prepared for cool weather – there could be snow on the ground for much of the year.

Start at the national park information office in the village of Crni Lug, signposted from the road from Rijeka to Delnice. Here you pay the park entrance fee and can pick up a leaflet about the walk.

The route is well signposted, with a series of information panels in Croatian and English explaining the geology, landscapes and wildlife. This gives you a good introduction to the mountain scenery of the Gorski Kotar, with the minimum of effort. The educational trail takes in meadows and streams, as well as man-made features such as a charcoal kiln and a hamlet of wooden and stone cottages. There is also a feeding post for animals, with beds of hay where dormice and squirrels shelter during the winter. Bears, wolves, lynx and pine martens all live in these forests and can occasionally be spotted on moonlit nights.

Stay on the waymarked trail to return to the information office at Crni Lug.

The lodge here serves hearty mountain fare such as venison goulash, mushroom soup and trout from the River Kupa.

Distance 4.2km (2.6 miles)
Time 1.5 hours
Start/end point Crni Lug 3D
Lunch Motel Risnjak (€€); Crni Lug; tel: 051 836133

SENJ

On your way to the Plitvice Lakes (➤ 46–47), stop in Senj to see the hilltop **castle,** the 16th-century base of the feared Uskok warriors and pirates in their battles against the Ottoman Turks. A museum inside the castle tells the story of the Uskoks, along with costumes and weapons, and conjures up the days when these pirates called this dramatic meeting between land and sea home.

www.tz-senj.hr

4E Bus from Rijeka

Stara Cesta 2; tel: 053 881068

Castle

May–Jun, Sep–Oct daily 10–6; Jul–Aug 10–9 Inexpensive

SVETVINČENAT

If you are driving along the old road from Pula to Pazin, stop off to take a look at one of the most attractive town squares in Istria. To one side is the 13th-century castle of the Grimani family, with its high walls and towers. Also around the square are the parish church, town hall and Venetian loggia, completing a harmonious ensemble. The oldest building is the 12th-century Romanesque Church of St Vincent, whose walls are covered with frescoes. Like other towns in inland Istria, Svetvinčenat has a thriving arts scene and concerts are held in the castle courtyard in summer.

2E Bus from Pula

Svetvinčenat 20; tel: 052 560349

UMAG

The northernmost resort on the Adriatic coast is just 40km (25 miles) from Trieste, making it popular with Italian visitors. In Croatia Umag is best known as the venue for the annual Croatia Open tennis tournament in late July. The old town, set on a narrow peninsula around a pretty bay, has almost been swallowed up by the tide of tourism around it. Savudrija, 8km (5 miles) north, is an attractive fishing port with pinewoods, rocky beaches and Croatia's oldest lighthouse, built in 1818, standing at right at the tip of the cape.

Just inland from Umag is the hilltop town of Buje, with a well-preserved medieval core and views from the ramparts to the sea. And from here you can discover the area's wine-growing traditions.

1D Bus from Pula and Poreč

Trgovačka 6; tel: 052 741 363

VODNJAN (DIGNANO)

In the 18th century Vodnjan was larger than Pula but these days it is a modest country town with Venetian Gothic palaces and Renaissance town houses lining its narrow streets and handsome main square. The parish Church of St Blaise dominates the town; at 63m (206ft), its bell tower is the tallest in Istria. The **collection of sacred art,** behind the altar, includes the mummified remains of three saints brought here from Venice for safekeeping in 1818. So far there has been no scientific explanation as to how the bodies have managed to be preserved rather than decomposing, so inevitably they have been attributed with miraculous powers.

2E Bus from Pula

Narodni Trg 3; tel: 052 511 700

Sacred Art Collection

Daily 9–7 in summer Expensive

VRSAR AND LIMSKI KANAL

The coastal town of Vrsar (Orsera) was previously the summer residence of the bishops of Poreč and their castle still stands above the town. Another regular visitor was the Italian adventurer and legendary seducer Giacomo Casanova (1725–98), whose memoirs record conquests here. Vrsar stands at the mouth of the Limski Kanal, a 10km (6-mile) fjord situated between thickly wooded cliffs, which is renowned thorughout Croatia for quality oysters. Local tour operators offer boat trips through the fjord in summer, which usually include a fish picnic and a visit to a pirate cave.

1E Bus from Poreč and Rovinj

Rade Končara 46; tel: 052 441746

HOTELS

MOTOVUN

Kaštel (€€)

Stylish family-run hotel on the main square, with a shady garden and roof terrace giving views across the Mirna Valley. The restaurant specializes in truffle dishes.

✉ Trg Andrea Antico 7 ☎ 052 681607; www.hotel-kastel-motovun.hr

NACIONALNI PARK BRIJUNI

Neptun-Istra (€€)

Enjoy Brijuni after the day trippers have left by staying at this harbourside hotel. Cycling, golf and tennis are available.

✉ Veli Brijun ☎ 052 525807; www.brijuni.hr

OPATIJA

Ika (€€)

If you can't afford Opatija prices, stay in this small beach hotel, an hour's walk along the promenade.

✉ Ulica Maršala Tita 16, Ika ☎ 051 291777; www.hotel-ika.hr

Kvarner-Amalia (€€)

Opened in 1884, this grand Habsburg-era hotel perfectly captures the faded elegance of *fin-de-siècle* Opatija, with its Crystal Ballroom and ornate classical facade.

✉ Ulica Tomašića 1 ☎ 051 271233; www.liburnia.hr

Mozart (€€€)

This stylish boutique hotel sets out to recreate Opatija's golden age, with Viennese-style salons and a piano bar. Most rooms have balconies facing the sea.

✉ Šetalište Maršala Tita 138 ☎ 051 718260; www.hotel-mozart.hr

Villa Ariston (€€)

Royalty and film stars have stayed at this elegant 19th-century villa, with beautiful flower gardens and stone terraces leading down to the seafront promenade.

✉ Šetalište Maršala Tita 179 ☎ 051 271379; www.villa-ariston.hr

POREČ

Fortuna (€€)

Large, modern hotel on the wooded island of Sveti Nikola, with views to the old town and shuttle boats from the harbour in summer.

✉ Otok Sveti Nikole ☎ 052 465 000; www.valmar.com 🕒 Apr–Oct

PULA

Riviera (€€)

This mustard-coloured relic from the Hapsburg era would not be out of place in Opatija or Zagreb. Not as grand as it looks but a convenient, central location.

✉ Splitska 1 ☎ 052 211166; www.arenaturist.hr

Scaletta (€€)

With 12 rooms in a town house beside the Roman arena, this stylish hotel makes a good choice in the centre of town.

✉ Ulica Flavijevska 26 ☎ 052 541025; www.hotel-scaletta.com

Valsabbion (€€)

Luxury 10-room hotel, overlooking a marina and pebble beach, with a beauty centre with hydromassage pool. The restaurant (➤ 184) is one of the best in Croatia.

✉ Pješčana Uvala 1X/26 ☎ 052 218033; www.valsabbion.hr 🕒 Feb–Dec

RIJEKA

Continental (€)

Old-style Austro-Hungarian hotel overlooking the river, a short walk from the city centre.

✉ Šetalište Andrije Kačića Miosica 1 ☎ 051 372008; www.jadran-hoteli.hr

ROVINJ

Adriatic (€€)

The oldest hotel in Rovinj occupies a prime position by the harbourside, with a cafe terrace and the best rooms having views out to sea.

✉ Obala Pina Budicina ☎ 052 803 510; www.maistra.com

Istra (€€)

Large, modern hotel on the island of Sveti Andrija, with regular shuttle boats to Rovinj. Swimming pools, tennis courts, spa centre and a pebble beach.

✉ Otok Sv Andrija ☎ 052 802500; www.maistra.com 🕓 Apr–Oct

Villa Angelo d'Oro (€€€)

Charming hotel in a restored 17th-century bishop's palace in the backstreets of the old town, with a peaceful garden, rooftop loggia and private yacht for rent.

✉ Via Svalba 38-42 ☎ 052 840502; www.rovinj.at

Villa Valdibora (€€€)

Four fully serviced apartments in a 17th-century baroque mansion, combining antique style with modern comforts such as computer, microwave and satellite TV. There are also two studio apartments and three twin/double rooms.

✉ Chiurco Silvano 8 ☎ 052 845040; www.valdibora.com

VODNJAN

Hotel Villa Letan (€€)

This modern hotel has sparse but clean and spacious rooms. Its conference facilities make it popular with the business crowd, however a restaurant serving up Istrian cuisine, outdoor tennis courts and a swimming pool are just some of the leisure facilities on offer.

✚ Peroj 450 ☎ 052 521009; www.hotel-letan.hr

RESTAURANTS

BUZET

Stara Oštarija (€€)

Exquisite truffle dishes including *frittata* (truffle omelette) and steak with truffles and truffles are also served with pasta and trout. The restaurant is perfectly sited in the heart of the old town of Buzet with views over a cliff.

✉ Ulika Petra Flega 5 ☎ 052 694003; www.stara-ostarija.com.hr
🕓 Wed–Mon 12–10

Toklarija (€€€)

One of the most expensive restaurants in Croatia serves top-quality Istrian produce in a restored oil mill above the Mirna Valley. Booking essential.

Sovinjsko Polje 11 (off the main road from Buzet to Motovun)
052 663031 Wed–Mon 1–10

HUM

Humska Konoba (€)

Small, rustic tavern in the tiny village of Hum, serving hearty dishes of pasta, truffles, goulash and roast lamb.

Hum 2 052 660005 Jun–Oct daily 11–10; Nov–Mar weekends only; Apr–May Tue–Sun

MOTOVUN

Kaštel (€€)

Generous portions of inland Istrian cuisine, such as pasta, goulash or steak with truffles, beneath the chestnut trees on the main square in summer.

Trg Andrea Antico 7 052 681607 Daily 8am–10pm

Mondo Konoba (€€)

This cosy *konoba* just outside the town gates serves up some of the best food in Istria. Here black truffles accompany everything from scrambled eggs and beef carpaccio to black truffle ravioli.

Ulica Barbacan 1 052 681791 Mar–Nov Wed–Mon 12:30–9:30

Pod Voltom (€€)

Brick-vaulted cellar beneath the arches at the entrance to the main square, specializing in fresh truffles in season, served with omelette, veal medallions or steak.

Trg Josefa Ressela 052 681923 Thu–Tue 12–11 (closed in winter)

Zigante (€€€)

The flagship restaurant of the Zigante truffle empire is found in the village of Livade. Truffles appear on the menu in various guises.

Livade 7 052 664302 Daily 12–11

OPATIJA

Amfora (€€)

This seafood restaurant is at the heart of Volosko's growing reputation as a gastronomic oasis. Lobster and tuna steak feature alongside staples such as squid and langoustines.

Črnikovica 4 051 701222, www.restaurant-amfora.com Daily 12–12

Ika (€€)

With tables on the terrace beside an attractive pebble beach, this restaurant makes a good lunchtime stop on the Lungomare coast walk from Opatija to Lovran.

Ulica Maršala Tita 16, Ika 051 291777 Daily 12–10

Istranka (€€)

Istrian classics like *maneštra* (vegetable soup) and *ombolo* (pork fillet with mushrooms) in a stone house just off the main street.

Ulica Bože Milanovića 2 051 2718357 Daily 10am–11pm

Le Mandrac (€€€)

Chic harbourside restaurant in the fishing village of Volosko, offering creative seafood dishes and modern Mediterranean cuisine on an alfresco terrace in summer.

Obala Frana Supila 10, Volosko 051 701357; www.lemandrac.com Daily 12–12

POREČ

Dvi Murve (€€)

This family-owned restaurant has been serving up Istrian specialities for over 30 years. Mussels, squid and lobsters from Kvarner and Dalmatia are among the highlights on the menu.

Grožnjanska 17 052 434115, May–Sep daily 12–12; Oct–Nov and Feb–Apr Wed–Mon 12–11

Nono (€)

Serves some of the best and biggest pizzas in Croatia, baked in a brick oven. Also steaks, seafood, pasta and excellent salads.

Zagrebačka 4 052 453088 Daily 12–12

PULA

Jupiter (€)

This bustling pizzeria serves up authentic thin-base Italian pizzas. The list of toppings is extensive and the pizzas themselves are cooked in a wood-fired oven. There is plenty of outdoor seating.

Casteropola 42 052 214333 Daily 9–11

Valsabbion (€€€)

Smart, exclusive restaurant in a boutique hotel overlooking the marina, with a choice of six-course tasting menus and a ten-course gastronomic menu based on fresh, seasonal "slow food".

Pješčana Uvala 052 218033; www.valsabbion.hr Daily 12–12 (closed in Jan)

ROVINJ

Al Gastaldo (€€)

Italian trattoria set just back from the harbour, offering pasta dishes, grilled vegetables and beef carpaccio throughout the year.

Ulica Iza Kasarne 14 052 814109 Daily 11–3, 6–11

Puntulina (€€€)

Fashionable wine bar and restaurant in a romantic setting, perched above the rocks with a balcony over the sea. Creative Istrian cuisine based on truffles and fresh fish.

Ulica Svetog Križa 38 052 813186 Mar–Oct daily 12–3, 6–11

Veli Jože (€€)

Rustic *konoba* by the harbour steps offering first-class Istrian cuisine both inside and out. Specialities include steak with truffles.

Ulica Svetog Križa 3 052 816337 Apr–Dec daily 11am–midnight

VODNJAN

Vodnjanka (€€)

Fresh seasonal produce, such as Istrian ham, cheese, asparagus, mushrooms and snails, at this cosy family-run restaurant.

Istarska 052 511435 Mon–Sat 11–11; also Sun 6pm–midnight in summer

VRSAR

Fjord (€€)

Busy restaurant with a large open-air terrace overlooking the jetty where the tour boats stop. The menu features fresh fish and oysters from the fjord.

✉ Limski Kanal, Sveti Lovreč ☎ 052 448223 🕐 Daily 12–11

SHOPPING

BUZET

Zigante Tartufi

Local farmer Giancarlo Zigante discovered the world's biggest white truffle in 1999 and he now owns a chain of shops selling truffle-based products and Istrian specialities. Fresh truffles are available in autumn; at other times you can buy preserved truffles, truffle oil and truffle paste. There is also an excellent selection of Istrian wines. The main shop is in Buzet, but there are branches in Buje, Grožnjan, Livade, Motovun and Pula.

✉ Trg Fontana ☎ 052 663340

GROŽNJAN

One of the biggest joys of a visit to the hilltop artists' village of Grožnjan is simply popping in to the numerous small galleries and boutiques where the local painters and craftspeople sell everything from original paintings to wall hangings crafted from stone.

ENTERTAINMENT

Valentino

Cool cocktail bar where you sit on silk cushions on the rocks, watching the sunset and listening to mellow music with your feet almost dangling in the sea.

✉ Ulica Svetog Križa 28, Rovinj ☎ 052 830683 🕐 Summer daily 6pm–3am

Zanzibar

One of the most stylish bars on the Istrian coast. The outdoor terrace has comfy seating and they mix a mean cocktail too.

✚ Obala Pina Budicina, Rovinj ☎ 052 813206

Index

Acknowledgements

The Automobile Association would like to thank the following photographers and companies for their assistance in the preparation of this book.

Abbreviations for the picture credits are as follows – (t) top; (b) bottom; (c) centre; (l) left; (r) right; (AA) AA World Travel Library

4l View from the Campanile, Rovinj, AA/P Bennett; **4c** Toll station, Zagreb-Split motorway, AA/J Smith; **4r** Roman amphitheatre, Pula, AA/P Bennett; **5l** ParkOld Town, Dubrovnik, Kuttig – Travel – 2/Alamy; **5c** Franciscan Monastery, Slavonski Brod, AA/P Bennett; **6/7** Skradin, AA/P Bennett; **8/9** St James Cathedral, Šibenik, AA/P Bennett; **10t** Coastal view, AA/P Bennett; **10cr** Alkar at Sinj, Croatian National Tourist Board; **10br-11** Dubrovnik, Croatian National Tourist Board; **11tl** Dubrovnik, Croatian National Tourist Board; **11cl** Rovinj, AA/P Bennett; **11cr** Clock tower, St Nicholas Church, Varaždin, AA/P Bennett; **12tr** Caf, Split, AA/J Smith; **12-13c** Fish Market, AA/P Bennett; **12bl** Cafeé, Zagreb, AA/P Bennett; **12br** Pumpkins, Zagorje, AA/P Bennett; **13t** Corn drying, AA/P Bennett; **13cr** Fish catch, AA/P Bennett; **14-15t** Food, AA/P Bennett; **14cr** Restaurant meal, AA/T Kelly; **14b** Market, Rijeka, AA/J Smith; **15tr** Custard tart, AA/J Smith; **15bl** Olive oil, AA/P Bennett; **15br** Spirits, AA/J Smith; **16cr** Cruise boat, AA/P Bennett; **16bl** Church, Samobor, AA/J Smith; **16bc** Balcony, Rovinj, AA/P Bennett; **17t** City walls, Dubrovnik, AA/P Bennett; **17b** Rovinj, AA/P Bennett; **18** Plitvice National Park, AA/P Bennett; **19cl** Café, Cavtat, AA/P Bennett; **19tr** Zlatni Rat beach, AA/P Bennett; **19b** Roman arena, Pula, AA/P Bennett; **20/21** Toll station, Zagreb-Split motorway, AA/J Smith; **24** Church of St Blaise, Dubrovnik, AA/J Smith; **26** Split airport, AA/J Smith; **27** Bus, AA/J Smith; **34/35** Roman arena, Pula, AA/P Bennett; **36** Diocletian's Palace, Split, AA/P Bennett; **37t** Clock Tower, Diocletian's Palace, Split, AA/J Smith; **37b** Diocletian's Palace, Split, AA/P Bennett; **38** St Mark's Church, Gornji Grad, Zagreb, AA/P Bennett; **39** Gornji Grad, Zagreb, AA/P Bennett; **40** City walls, Dubrovnik, AA/P Bennett; **41** City walls, Dubrovnik, AA/P Bennett; **42** Hvar, AA/P Bennett; **43** Hvar, AA/P Bennett; **44** Mljet, Jonathan Chinnery; **45** Lizard, Mljet, Jonathan Chinnery; **46** Plitvice National Park, AA/P Bennett; **46/47c** Plitvice National Park, AA/P Bennett; **48** Arena, Pula, AA/P Bennett; **49t** Pula Arena, Roman amphitheatre, imagebroker/Alamy; **49b** Arena, Pula, AA/P Bennett; **50b** Rovinj, AA/P Bennett;

51t Rovinj, Photoshot Holdings Ltd/Alamy; **52l** Varaždin, AA/P Bennett; **52-53c** Varaždin, AA/P Bennett; **55** Zlatni Rat beach, AA/P Bennett; **56–57** Dubrovnik Old Town, Kuttig – Travel – 2/Alamy; **59** Cafe, Rovinj, Ian Dagnall/Alamy; **60/61** Flotilla of yachts, Southern Dalmatia, AA/P Bennett; **63** Carp pool, AA/P Bennett; **64** Lungomare walk, Opatija, AA/P Bennett; **65tr** Lungomare walk, Opatija, AA/P Bennett; **65b** Lungomare walk, Opatija, AA/P Bennett; **66-67** Beli, Cres Island AA/P Bennett; **68** Dubrovnik Summer Festival, Damil Kalogjera/Dubrovnik Summer Festival; **71** Paklenica National Park, AA/P Bennett; **72-73** Franciscan Monastery, Slavonski Brod, AA/P Bennett; **75** Dubrovnik, AA/P Bennett; **76** Well, Dominican Monastery, Dubrovnik, AA/J Smith; **77** Franciscan Monastery, Dubrovnik, AA/P Bennett; **78** Cathedral, Dubrovnik, AA/P Bennett; **79** Rector's Palace, Dubrovnik, AA/J Smith; **80tl** Stradun, Dubrovnik, AA/J Smith; **80-81t** Church of St Blaise, Dubrovnik, AA/J Smith; **81bl** St John's Fort, Dubrovnik, AA/P Bennett; **82cl** Onofrio fountain, Dubrovnik, AA/P Bennett; **82br** Detail, Onofrio fountain, Dubrovnik, AA/P Bennett; **82-83c** Stradun, Dubrovnik, AA/P Bennett; **84** Cafe, Cavtat, AA/P Bennett; **85** Lopud, Elafiti Islands, AA/J Smith; **86** Lokrum ferry boat, AA/P Bennett; **87** Trsteno Arboretum, AA/P Bennett; **91** Yachts, Trogir, AA/P Bennett; **92** Sarcophagus detail, Archaeological Museum, Split, AA/J Smith; **93** Ethnographic Museum, Split, AA/J Smith; **94** Mestrovic Gallery, Split, AA/J Smith; **95** Cathedral of St Domnius, Diocletian's Palace, Split, AA/J Smith; **96** Bol harbour, Brac Island, AA/P Bennett; **97** Korčula, AA/P Bennett; **98t** Kornati Island's AA/P Bennett; **98bl** Makarska, AA/P Bennett; **99** Makarska Riviera, AA/P Bennett; **100–101** Krka National Park, AA/P Bennett; **102** Roman amphitheatre, Salona, AA/P Bennett; **103** Šibenik, AA/P Bennett; **104–105** Trogir, AA/P Bennett; **104bl** St Lawrence Cathedral, Trogir, AA/P Bennett; **105b** St Dominic, Trogir, AA/P Bennett; **106** Mosaic, Franciscan Monastery, Vis, AA/J Smith; **107** Boat, Zadar, AA/J Smith; **108** Zrmanja river, Obrovac, JadroFoto/Alamy; **109** Croatian national flag, AA/P Bennett; **119** Gornji Grad, Zagreb, AA/P Bennett; **120** Gornji Grad, Zagreb, AA/P Bennett; **121** Bust of Ivan Meštrović, Meštrović Gallery, Zagreb, AA/P Bennett; **122** Botanical Gardens, Zagreb, AA/P Bennett; **123** Botanical Gardens, Zagreb, AA/P Bennett; **124** Mirogoj Cemetery, Zagreb, AA/P Bennett; **125t** Mirogoj Cemetery, Zagreb, AA/P Bennett; **125cr** Mirogoj Cemetery, Zagreb, AA/P Bennett; **126** Cathedral view, Zagreb, AA/P Bennett; **127** View from Burglars' Tower, Zagreb, AA/P Bennett; **128** Maksimirski Perivoj, Zagreb, Courtesy of Zagreb Tourist Board; **129** Cable car to Sljeme, Courtesy of Zagreb Tourist Board; **130** Exhibit, Museum of the City of Zagreb, AA/P Bennett; **130–131** *The Bather* painting by Renoir, Mimara Museum, Zagreb, AA/P Bennett; **131br** Venetian glass, Mimara Museum, Zagreb, AA/P Bennett; **132** The Gallery of Old Masters, Zagreb, AA/P Bennett; **133t** Statue of Jelačić, Trg Bana Jelačića, Zagreb, AA/P Bennett; **133b** Cafés, Trg Bana Jelačića, Zagreb, AA/P Bennett; **134bl** Detail, Gornji Grad, Zagreb, AA/P Bennett; **134–135c** Tower of Lotrščak, Gornji Grad, Zagreb, AA/P Bennett; **135tr** Detail, Gornji Grad, Zagreb, AA/P Bennett; **135br** Dolac Market, Zagreb, AA/P Bennett; **136** Čakovec, AA/P Bennett; **137** Cathedral of St Peter, Đakovo, AA/P Bennett; **138** Kopački Rit, AA/P Bennett; **139** Kopački Rit, AA/P Bennett; **140** Statue of Tito, Kumrovec, AA/P Bennett; **141** Kumrovec, AA/P Bennett; **142** Lonjsko Polje, AA/J Smith; **143** Church of Our Lady of the Snows, Marija Bistrica, AA/P Bennett; **144bl** Bell tower, Church of St Michael, Osijek, AA/P Bennett; **144–145** Plague Monument, Osijek, AA/P Bennett; **145cr** Trg Kralja Tomislava, Samobor, AA/J Smith; **146** Castle, Trakošćan, AA/P Bennett; **147** Castle, Trakošćan, AA/P Bennett; **148** Castle, Veliki Tabor, AA/P Bennett; **149** War-damaged buildings, Vukovar, AA/P Bennett; **159** Rab, AA/P Bennett; **160** Groznjan, James Russell travel/Alamy; **161** Buzet, AA/P Bennett; **162** Hum, AA/P Bennett; **163** Krk, AA/P Bennett; **164** Brijuni, Milan Babić/Croatian National Tourist Board; **165t** Roman glue factory ruins, Veli Brijuni, AA/P Bennett; **165b** Brijuni Isles excursion, AA/P Bennett; **166** Villa Angiolina, Opatija, AA/P Bennett; **167t** Detail, Pazin Castle, AA/J Smith; **167b** Pazin, AA/J Smith; **168t** Cafe, Poreč, AA/P Bennett; **168b** Euphrasius Basilica, Poreč, AA/P Bennett; **169** Euphrasius Basilica, Poreč, AA/P Bennett; **170-171** Bell tower, Rab, AA/P Bennett; **171cr** Cathedral of St Vitus, Rijeka, AA/J Smith; **172** Risnjak National Park, AA/P Bennett; **173t** Risnjak National Park, AA/P Bennett; **173b** Risnjak National Park, AA/P Bennett; **174-175t** Nehaj Castle, Senj, AA/J Smith; **176** Umag, AA/P Bennett; **177** Tower of St Blaise, Vodnjan, AA/P Bennett; **178** Vrsar, Images-Europa / Alamy.

Every effort has been made to trace the copyright holders, and we apologise in advance for any unintentional omissions or errors. We would be happy to apply any corrections in the following edition of this publication.

Sight Locator Index

This index relates to the maps on the covers. We have given map references to the main sights of interest in the book. Grid references in italics indicate sights featured on town plans. Some sights within towns may not be plotted on the maps.

Dear Reader

Your comments, opinions and recommendations are very important to us. Please help us to improve our travel guides by taking a few minutes to complete this simple questionnaire.

You do not need a stamp (unless posted outside the UK). If you do not want to cut this page from your guide, then photocopy it or write your answers on a plain sheet of paper.

Send to: **The Editor, AA World Travel Guides, FREEPOST SCE 4598, Basingstoke RG21 4GY.**

Your recommendations...

We always encourage readers' recommendations for restaurants, nightlife or shopping – if your recommendation is used in the next edition of the guide, we will send you a **FREE AA Guide** of your choice from this series. Please state below the establishment name, location and your reasons for recommending it.

____

____

____

____

____

____

Please send me **AA Guide** ______________________________

About this guide...

Which title did you buy?

AA ____________________________________

Where did you buy it? ______________________________

When? m m / y y

Why did you choose this guide? __________________________

____

____

____

____

Did this guide meet your expectations?

Exceeded ☐ Met all ☐ Met most ☐ Fell below ☐

Were there any aspects of this guide that you particularly liked? ________________

____

____

____

continued on next page...

Is there anything we could have done better? ______________________

____

____

____

About you...

Name (*Mr/Mrs/Ms*) ______________________

Address ______________________

____

______________________ Postcode ____________

Daytime tel nos ______________________

Email ______________________

Please only give us your mobile phone number or email if you wish to hear from us about other products and services from the AA and partners by text or mms, or email.

Which age group are you in?

Under 25 ☐ 25–34 ☐ 35–44 ☐ 45–54 ☐ 55–64 ☐ 65+ ☐

How many trips do you make a year?

Less than one ☐ One ☐ Two ☐ Three or more ☐

Are you an AA member? Yes ☐ No ☐

About your trip...

When did you book? m m / y y When did you travel? m m / y y

How long did you stay? ______________________

Was it for business or leisure? ______________________

Did you buy any other travel guides for your trip? ______________________

If yes, which ones? ______________________

____

____

Thank you for taking the time to complete this questionnaire. Please send it to us as soon as possible, and remember, you do not need a stamp (*unless posted outside the UK*).

The information we hold about you will be used to provide the products and services requested and for identification, account administration, analysis, and fraud/loss prevention purposes. More details about how that information is used is in our privacy statement, which you'll find under the heading "Personal Information" in our terms and conditions and on our website: www.theAA.com. Copies are also available from us by post, by contacting the Data Protection Manager at AA, Fanum House, Basing View, Basingstoke, Hampshire RG21 4EA.

We may want to contact you about other products and services provided by us, or our partners (by mail, telephone or email) but please tick the box if you DO NOT wish to hear about such products and services from us by mail, telephone or email. ☐